Loaded For Bear

Stockton Todd Holden

Printed in the United States of America
First Printing, 2017

ISBN 978-0-9860911-2-4

Cairn of Quartz Publishing
315 East Broadway
Bel Air, MD 21014

Also by Stockton Todd Holden:
Son, You Turn A Good Phrase (www.createspace.com/5166256)
Twists and Turns In The Road (www.createspace.com/6544228)

Design, Production, and Editing
Patrick Wallis

Marketing and Communications Director
Barbara Szymanski

Personal Assistant and Fact Checker to Mr. Holden
Mina Jean Holden-Horn

Some comments worth sharing...

Todd, I read your book and like to call it your Rustica Pond Book. H. D. Thoreau would find it most interesting. Vignettes of everyday life that sometimes fade from memory but which you so skillfully bring to the surface.

What you wrote about picking up those field rocks was great. Being a farm boy myself I have picked up my share of stones. I never really minded it as we ambled along on those sunny days. Never in a rush like getting the hay bales in before the approaching storm or trying the get all the ripened apples picked before they fell to the ground. I would never be able to write anything interesting about picking up rocks but with your "heaving and belching on the fields"....I get it.

Todd, you turn a good phrase.

Emerson Hoopes, Arizona

* * *

Having read Todd's books and having enjoyed them thoroughly, I have come to understand their importance...this importance lies in the truth telling and the historical contents as well as the humanity deeply portrayed in them. This is a thread that runs throughout each and every one of his stories and which highlights his unique way of seeing his world and the people who reside in it. There are also much loved animals and creatures who live in this world. He is a man of great depth of feeling and, more importantly, he has an amazing ability to let us become a part of this world, as well, through his story telling.

Pamela Berkley Rich, Baltimore, Maryland

I read your book this weekend and felt I was back at home. Loved the cadence of your words. And the continuing theme of loss and transition was particularly compelling for me.

Lynne Tobin, Vermont

* * *

If you don't have time to pull up a rocking chair on a wide wooden porch with an ice cold beer in summer....or a steaming mug of cocoa on a winter's morn...If you can't quite make it out to your dear friend's porch for some acutely observed and magically unfolding tales, then Todd Holden's books are the next best thing. Summer tales and winter tales, autumn and springtime too, yours to delve into in this series of books that will make you feel that chair rocking gently beneath you, as each story carries you further out. You'll come for the twists and unexpected turns many of these tales take and you'll stay for the vivid heart you can feel beating in each and every word.

Donna Sherman, Baltimore, Maryland

As much as Todd Holden is an oral historian, so must these captured vignettes remain sealed in time and presented in the pages of this book as they first appeared in that wonderful, local paper,  *The Delta Star*. There were discussions about updating particulars – of buildings gone and loved ones passed on – but somehow it felt like it would be a disservice to the original spirit with which these observations were penned. We also thought about adding codas to every story as a way of explaining facts, such as the Roller Rink no longer being in operation or providing a current update on the health of the pups of Rustica.

Setting all that aside, relax with this book when you too can suspend time, if just for a moment, and let these stories remind you of days gone by, impart to you a few of life's lessons in respecting nature, and engage you with tales of adventure and woe. These recollections speak locally, but have a much wider appeal than any physical boundary.

Working with Todd has been a necessary adventure, for both of us. Where we've struggled with edits, perspectives and final thoughts has been more than made up for by the magic created in the retelling of these stories. Whether tales of adventure in the private preserve at Rustica or further exploits deep in the heart of Delta, each of these stories tells the truth, offers an observation, and gives a gift that will do your heart good. Enjoy!

Patrick Wallis

We would be remiss if we did not take note of the tremendous contributions of Barbara Szymanski, our editor, book and web site manager, marketing director, you name it. Brought in as a critical extra pair of eyes to go through the book, Barb quickly has become crucial to the operation, handling book signings, web and blog inquiries, and many things this 78-year old knows nothing about. Thank you Barbara, for your myriad of skills, tireless efforts and an endless reserve of patience in putting up with an excitable, sometimes contrary, but always open to suggestions kind of guy.

Todd Holden

Navigator

A s a little girl growing up in Leeswood, I spent a lot of time with my Dad.

"Hey, 'Birdlegs,' want to go for a drive?"

I would jump at the chance to be his navigator (no GPS, only an unfolded SHA map and a highlighter). Taking a drive with my Dad meant getting away from my younger brother, who could be annoying as heck. It also meant that I'd get to help him during one of his photo shoots or that we'd grab an ice cream from the Arctic Circle (if the road led us in that direction).

I love to drive, and I'm pretty sure it's because of my Dad. Windows down, 8 track tapes loaded, me singing at the top of my lungs, some conversation and many laughs (usually after my dad performed a 'silent but deadly'). He'd have a job to do, photos to take, a covered bridge, an accident, a new store, a wedding, lots of weddings.

STH

Sometimes he'd just want to have a companion to go with him when he went to visit a friend or to get new fish for his aquarium. Other times, he needed me as his assistant to lug his camera equipment or sit in the pew of the church to make sure nothing happened to his stuff. Sometimes, I even helped arrange the wedding party for him as they posed for pictures after the ceremony. He made me feel important and needed, like an adult.

We always took back roads. Queue up John Denver, Neil Young, The Beatles, Jim Croce. We would sing, talk, and enjoy the ride with music. Always something magical about my Dad and music.

He kept a journal in his glove compartment...even gave me my first diary. He always said to write down my thoughts, my ideas, my observations, gas mileage, clever quotes.

He told me it was good to get your thoughts out through paper and pen. Often times, he'd pull over and take out his little journal, slide off the rubber band, and jot down a line or two. Sometimes he'd talk out loud about what he was writing and I'd give him my two cents....maybe there are a few quotes from me in those old journals...you never know.

I don't really remember where he would write before my parents converted our breezeway into his office. I'm guessing the studio. And I don't remember a typewriter at home (only the old black Royal he later gave to me).

STH

I think he mostly wrote in long hand on yellow legal pads. He had a mug full of Cross pens, felt tips, and sharpened pencils. At home, in the newly designed office, he had privacy, where he could close the door and meditate, write, read, rearrange the plants in his fish tank, meet with friends, listen to music, or watch tv.

It was a comfortable room and it was his...when my parents weren't home it was a good place for me to watch tv, without fighting with Sam about how Little House on the Prairie was far better than Batman. For the most part, however, it was off limits to me and Sam. There would be wafts of 'incense' burning many nights... and I'd stay away, in my bedroom, writing down my favorite lyrics to songs, reading, doing homework, or singing along to the 45s playing on my stereo. Like father, like daughter, only minus the 'incense' (I couldn't stand the smell!).

There's something to say about going on a long drive, along the back roads of Harford County, breathing in the sweet aroma of freshly mown hay, listening to my Dad ramble about the past, stories of his life, people he's met, and life lessons (really, they were lectures, but that's for another time), and just maybe those drives with me by his side helped him to navigate that Cross pen across the yellow pages of the legal pad when we got home.

Next time I'll tell you about other things my Dad liked to do on our drives...hitchhikers come to mind.

Mina Jean Holden-Horn

Alpha Jean Todd Holden

S he was my mother, through thick and thin. I loved her as children will and she loved me as only a mother can. Because we were both strong-willed we had rough patches some times, not all the time...near the end we made peace and for that I am grateful.

STH

She was tough, from North Carolina, with her youth spent in Manitou Springs, Colorado. She learned to shoot rattlesnakes and was a tomboy. She and her mom, Eva Grace McKnight Todd shared tending to her father Carl Todd, who was stricken with tuberculosis and literally sent west to die...at the time it was the way things were done with some diseases.

He became well, as much as he could and the family returned to Maryland. Mr. Todd was a cattleman and, together with his brother Ross Todd, operated a general store in Fountain Green, now the site of a Royal Farms.

Mom taught me to shoot a rifle, catch a snake, love nature and all manner of wildlife. She would 'camp out' in our yard with me and my younger brother, Brian... tilting two Adirondack chairs together and draping a huge army blanket over them...our shelter from the storm.

When my brother died at a young age, everything changed. My dad said to me one day, 'We've died too, son' and I, too, felt the pain. Brian's death really affected my mother and losing a child, as many of us know, can be devastating...for her it was...in oh so many ways. After dad died in 1994, I would learn how much he did for her, how much he loved her, and I did what I could for her. I wanted to make her happy and live comfortably.

STH

I would drive her to Florida for her winter stay in Vero Beach. Those long drives south in the car were the best of times...something about driving with someone really opens the conversations up. We both loved a practical joke and reminisced about some of them on the long drives. Just being together meant a lot to both of us. We both had endured loss, with both dad and Brian, but we still had each other.

I was sitting with her when she died in her own bed in 1999...I was relieved that she was out of her suffering. Surely, her life had been filled with enough suffering for a dozen women.

Lately, I have had dreams of her, little snippets surge into my sleep and I wake with a smile for her and me.

So, Jean, mom, this book is for you...you encouraged me to leave the newspaper business and strike out on my own...it was good advice...thank you mom...you did good...I hope I did good enough for you....

========= 30 =========

Photo Credit...Sam Holden was asked by his newspaper editor for an image depicting the 'elderly being armed during these turbulent times.' Immediately, he thought of his grandmother, Jean Todd Holden, who was 80 and in the final stages of colon cancer. She was honored to do the shoot, in her living room, with a Ruger 44 magnum with bullets...on loan from the Robert Ewers Collection. She began loading the weapon, Sam started shooting...luckily, she didn't...Sam had his cover for the article...1998, Bel Air.

Rustica

In many of my stories mention is made of the 'Walden Project'...a way of life taken in part from the writings of Henry David Thoreau...so it came to be in 1984, a small, 24-acre parcel in the northwest corner of my parents farm, Southampton, I built a passive-solar home...literally a 'house within a house'...energy efficient.

My parents and my grandfather purchased Southampton in 1953 from a respected farmer and cattleman, William Amoss and his wife, Ellen.

I was raised on this farm of 557 acres with my brother, Brian. It was a dairy farm. We had crops of soybean, alfalfa, corn and sorghum. We fed the registered herd of Holstein Friesians from the crops we raised. There were three tenant houses on the farm.

When I was given the chance to build a home, my wife Ann and I went to the site to visually lay out where it was to be built...on a ridge with slopes tapering to Bynum run and Wysong branch to the north. As we stood there on this beautiful knoll, a barn-swallow repeatedly flew around us. Seems we had kicked up some insects as we walked around in the hayfield and we had disturbed dinner.

STH

It was a great moment for us...we would no longer
live in Leeswood, in the rancher we had built on
Southern drive...this would be a home right out of
Mother Earth News, a salt-box style home, heated by
wood, without a basement...as my mom said, 'It's not
my cup of tea.'

Later, that moment when the barn swallow flew
over us was taken as a sign, a good omen...when I later
looked up the ornithological name of a barn swallow I
learned it was 'hirundo rustica'...thus we decided then
and there to honor the bird that welcomed us on the
knoll that spring evening...since then our home place
has been called Rustica.

Todd Holden

Groundhog Karma

Ever since I was a kid living on a dairy farm and helping with the chores, I learned that groundhog holes in the hay fields were a nuisance to the equipment. A tractor tire or wagon loads of hay often were out of commission when they encountered a groundhog hole. These outdoor rodents had a way of disrupting life on the farm and once they took over territory, they were just as belligerent to keep it.

So we were allowed to shoot groundhogs after the fields were cut and baled. Mostly, we used 22-caliber rifles and sometimes, not all the time, we were permitted to carry a rifle on the tractor when we pulled wagons. It seemed the groundhogs were less suspicious when a tractor pulling a hay wagon lumbered across a big field, where there might have been half a dozen holes. I recall bagging a few and missing some. I'll never forget their faces as they stared back at me just before dropping down a hole.

As time went on, the groundhogs seemed less a problem than the cost of fuel to put a crop in the ground, then pray for rain and hope for a good harvest. But for a time, doing battle with these pesky scoundrels took priority and served as a pleasant diversion from the hard work we performed.

STH

Many years removed from the farm life, but not all that different in some respects, I live my days at Rustica Wilderness where all manner of critters live and visit. The lane coming into Rustica is almost a quarter mile long, half of which goes through woods, directly from the main road. You then emerge into the open wood margin and soybean fields. Here's where the 'Groundhog Karma' comes in and the old field wars on the farm with these fat creatures comes to mind.

Often, when I set out to run errands, all three pups go into a frenzy to ride with me, so I've put a big horse blanket across the back seat and let them come along. After the stops at the post office, Tommy Weaver's shop, the doctor's office and whatever else there is to do I head home and the anticipation builds in the backseat.

At the main road, where the lane begins, I let the pups out and they are in full stride in about 10 feet. They scamper through the skunk cabbage, across the little stream and back and forth across the gravel lane. Excitement is barely contained, for both them and myself, with the anticipation of the chase...of rousting a groundhog, squirrel or chipmunk.

They arrive at the house ready for a big drink of cool water and then a stretch in the shade or sun depending on the temperature. Frisco may join in on a chase, but for the most part is along for the ride and just as content running with the others.

STH

Some days, when it's raining I leave the pups at home, since it's a bit muddy in and out of the Expedition. Sometimes it's a sunny day, but I have lots of things to do and it's too hot in the car for them. As if on cue, on the days when the pups stay home, sure enough one or two groundhogs run across the lane, from the field to the woods. Sometimes they run along the lane then dart into the woods where the dens are.

Why is it then, when the pups are with me...no groundhogs? When they are not with me, the little buggers are dancing and taunting me with a 'ha ha, you can't get me' attitude. Oh yes, I'm reminded of the farm days and my prior battles with the little kingpins.

Shucks! Groundhog Karma deprives me of the fun of the chase, the antics of two pups tearing through the gravel in hot pursuit of the furry vegetarian. This is not to say they haven't scored a time or two, because both Dude and Chester have, big time.

Dude usually runs the perimeter of the yard around the house and will spook a groundhog munching unaware of the persistent Dudester lurking nearby. He also 'goes to ground' in the natural attack mode of the purebred Jack Russell.

My only worry is that in a duel, I could lose Dude or Chester in a split second if one of the claws on the groundhog catches them in the throat. That's a fear that anyone who hunts with Jacks has to weigh in their mind of whether or not to hunt them. If you let them do what

Tempting karma, Chester delivers a gift. Photo by Todd Holden.

comes naturally, you will let them hunt and watch carefully on their behalf.

So far this season, there have been no encounters along the lane. Chester did catch one and surprised even himself I think. It's a real battle of wits and for the most part, the groundhogs are winning.

That's just fine with Dude, he enjoys the 'ride and the chase' and remains a nonchalant little guy when it comes to the curse of 'Groundhog Karma' and knows that patience will get him another shot.

Last week, I was heading up the lane alone after having left all of the pups at the house. As I came into the clearing there were two brave groundhogs on the side of the lane up on their hind legs looking square at me. I swear the one on the left looked exactly like the one I missed with the rifle back at the farm...always good to recognize a little karma.

========== 30 ==========

STH

Sunday Mornings

Anyone who's read my column knows I like to take Sunday drives. Sundays long ago were spent visiting family and friends, putting the time aside to give thanks. Taking that ride in the country these days may have adapted to the times, but it is still a great pleasure of mine.

Sunday cruises with Frisco, The Dude and Chester usually wind up in or around Delta, Coulsontown, Bangor, and then Darlington. There are many routes and the roads often reveal new adventures and lessons...from time to time and season to season.

Today I heard a name from Kenkaid that I had not heard before, Billy Booker, who passed away about six months ago. "He could do nearly anything, one of the kindest people you would ever meet," Kenkaid said. He told me there were a million stories about Booker. The problem was that on this particular day, he couldn't remember any of them. "Have no fear," he said. He'd jot them down and fill me in later.

After I left Kenkaid's, I decided to do a little research on Booker and I went to church. Many members of the congregation catty-corner from the Welsh Church on Atom road were heading to their cars as I pulled onto the parking lot. A man who called himself 'Fox' said

STH

he knew Booker well, as did a lady with Fox. But, being
Easter Sunday, everyone was headed to family dinners,
thus some Booker stories will filter in as time passes.

Yes, this is how stories are built, edited and written.
Just letting you all in on the process. An interesting
recollection from a pal sometimes opens up whole new
accounts of a local character. The stories about Bud
Lloyd and Kenny Cantler came about this way, and other
names mentioned in that research will lead to other
stories of interesting people from the area.

The more I look, listen, and discover, the more
characters I find. Not shady characters mind you,
although I'm sure the area has a few of them. What
interests me more are the folks who made their mark in a
good way.

Before I left Kenkaid's, we recalled some of the
'gooders' who have passed on that touched the lives of
both of us. Simple, under-the-radar folks who go about
life with a right-minded spirit, fine moral fiber and
respect that goes both ways. Folks I wish I had gotten
to know and now must rely on word of mouth to piece
together their story. Some have passed on to the realm of
'folk lore' or 'folk hero.'

These people are not the big time politicians or
the social pillars of our society. On the contrary, they
are quiet, hard working, honest folks who go about
living their lives in a respectable manner. They help
friends in need, they don't stand for lying or dishonesty,

STH

and they have friends that work as hard as they do. Their good deeds often go unnoticed, mainly because these individuals don't need the recognition, just the satisfaction of doing what they think is right.

You know people who fit this bill...they stand out in their quietness. They perform their work diligently and with purpose in mind. They go the extra mile, they do their work as good as they can, without cutting corners.

A few of the famed Delta Crew. l-r Mac Lloyd, Bob Lloyd, Bob Pruitt, Todd Holden and Danny McLaughlin. Photo by Pat Wallis.

STH

Maybe that's why I like getting up on Sundays and loading the pups, and once in a great while a pal, for a little excursion into the country. I don't like to cut corners myself and well...around these parts, you just never know what or who you'll learn about when you turn the corner.

When we come upon a story about someone who merits our attention, someone who lived and breathed moral fiber long before the phrase was popular, we become curious about the things they did and how they lived. Perhaps a little of their magic rubs off on us and instills in us the desire to do good things too. Keeps us all learning.

========= 30 =========

Morning Is Not Broken...It Fixes

A customary morning greeting. Photo by Pat Wallis.

Sitting on the deck, shortly after dawn, the air feels better than at any other time of the day. First sounds heard are the songs of the bluebirds, several of them. It pleases me to no end.

Where the nests are I do not know, because the bluebird boxes are mostly filled twigs from house wrens. These birds often don't build their own nests, they merely block any other birds like bluebirds and chickadees from nesting there. I am not a fan of house wrens, so when I see the twigs sticking out of the bluebird box, it's cleaned out immediately, and a stick placed in the box to temporarily deter the wrens from persistent rebuilding.

STH

True, this also keeps the bluebirds out, but the chickadees can still get in and build their nifty 'double-layered' nests of grass and moss. This is just one of many intricacies of living with the nature around us, and being aware when we can lend a hand to the less aggressive creatures who share the land.

Listening to the singing of the bluebirds this morning I wonder where they are nesting. Likely in a tree where a limb has blown off, leaving that little hole where the cavity nesting birds love to raise a family. So it is the bluebirds are doing what comes naturally without my help. The late mentor, Wilson Ford, tutored me early on about the benefits and plight of the eastern bluebird. We both walked many miles installing and then maintaining bluebird boxes all over the county. They were great times with Wilson...

Now it's just me, here, listening to the gentle song of the bluebird. Feels good to take it all in...the early part of the day, a second cup of Chock Full O'Nuts and the pups milling about, wondering what I'm gonna do next. Funny thing is, I'm not sure myself.

Another thought comes to mind...watching the barn swallows ranging back and forth over the freshly planted field corn, other birds I can't really identify near the pond, still others calling out from the woods...the thought occurs to me...this is what I'm supposed to be doing at this moment.

STH

Rustica benches. Photo by Pat Wallis.

It's hard to feel or think we've earned this...but we who are up in years have earned what a little thing like this simple pleasure of the early day brings to us. The chores as they are, were done a day or two ago. Today, it's allowable to sit back and take in the spontaneous panorama of life around me, without me being involved in helping make it happen.

Sit back, relax, bub, just let things unfold the way they're meant to be. It's that appreciation today that comes to mind. I'm a lucky guy. For sure...and some times, not all the time, all I have to do is act naturally.

STH

As the sun rises I get up to move with the day, putter with intent. The song of the bluebirds and now an early Buck Owens song keeps me moving.

Later in the morning, Gary Rinehart comes by with a four-foot plus healthy black snake he rescued. Gary is terrified of snakes, but he will not kill them, which is good. He hands me the feed sack with the snake, asking where I'm gonna turn it loose. The tool shed looks like a good spot, mice in there, so that's what I do.

All this in one sweet morning...surely, I am a lucky guy!

========= 30 =========

Reading Another 'Old Bottle'

Ever since way back when Gene Streett, proprietor of Boyd and Fulford's Drug Store in Bel Air told me that many of the old time remedies are not the same as they used to be, I've been intrigued with what they used to be, not so much what they are now. So it was I entered Boyd and Fulford's the other day looking for an old remedy.

I have always sworn by a remedy my Grandma Holden used for infections, splinters and other blistery stuff that kids get. Her remedy was 'Black Iodex Ointment' and it was black like tar, sort of like black Vaseline, with all kinds of ingredients to help heal a bad cut or sore.

Black Iodex Ointment has been around for many years and is made today, but that day Gene told me, "The old black Iodex ain't what it used to be Todd. You see, the government has made the manufacturer change the ingredients, sort of toning it down, and now it isn't half as good as it used to be." I still bought the little vessel of it, and used it, but to be real, Neosporin and Bacitracin ointments are much better than the new version of Iodex.

There's always a cut or scrape on me somewhere from stuff I do around Rustica, and that's the best way to keep any of them from becoming infected and a bigger problem.

STH

So it came to pass the other day I was looking for alcohol and cotton balls to wipe away scratches from hauling multi-flora roses. Then, in the 'medicine drawer' I noticed a bottle of 'Campho-Phenique'...a name many of you likely have never heard of.

I wondered if it was still sold. This bottle was very old, and I began to read the information on the container. Always a good habit to follow, but it dawned on me how interestingly things were worded back in the day.

> "Campho-Phenique®...liquid, plastic bottle, pain-relieving antiseptic... stops hurting and itching...starts healing sores, cuts, burns, insect bites, fever blisters and cold sores."

The little brown bottle contained '3/4 fluid oz.'

> "Forms a soothing, germ-killing shield to help speed healing of cuts, minor burns, blisters, abrasions, scrapes, razor nicks, chafed or irritated skin, itchy bites from chiggers, mosquitoes, sand fleas and black flies."

I would imagine it wouldn't work on those big city bed bugs, but who knows?

STH

"Ingredients — Phenol 4.7% (w,w) and
Camphor 10.8% (w.w). Also contains
Eucalyptus Oil, Light mineral oil."

Manufactured by Winthrop Consumer
Products, Division of Sterling
Drug, Inc., New York, N.Y. 10016.

Here's the kicker, on the box that said the product
expired 'May-1991' was this warning...

"For households without young
children---this product size does
not have a child guard cap."

How's that for straight information? No fooling
around there.

I opened the little brown bottle, sniffed it, smelled
o.k. to me, and so, tonight I'll get to the multi-flora
abrasions and see how it works...heck it's worth a try.

Besides, it was great fun to read the label...and learn
there was not 'filler' in the ingredients. Rare! That's
the problem when you get close to 73...some of the 'tried
and true remedies' aren't around anymore, or just aren't
the same anymore...maybe it's too much government
intervention...like messing with things that aren't broke.

STH

Seems to be a lot of that, and it's a waste of time and money...not to mention, fixing things that aren't broke, well, just breaks them.

Black Iodex Ointment and the early Neosporin worked fine, and no one died from using them...not to my knowledge...but folks out there, in high places...who are no smarter than you or me, make decisions that are plain brainless. They make decisions that they tell us are all about protecting us, keeping everyone safe. To be honest, I really didn't know I was in that much danger.

Now, I'm not advocating a major repeal of safety regulations...obviously, we need to protect ourselves from jamming a tube of black ointment deep into our ear canals. Enough intervention into our lives, though. All I can say is, I'm going to use this bottle of Campho-Phenique® rather sparingly.

========= 30 =========

Doc Hunt Would Be Proud

A glove isn't always necessary when handling a docile black snake.
But, it doesn't hurt. Photo by Gary Rinehart.

I t's usually when you're trying to do the right
thing that things sometimes go a little awry...and
such was the case the other day when my friend Gary
Rinehart caught a good sized black snake at his home
on Goat Hill Road near Creswell. Gary isn't particularly
fond of snakes...not quite as bad as 'Screamin' Mackie
Lloyd, but nonetheless, he prefers to bring them over to
my place, rather than kill them.

STH

That's a good thing. All snakes are welcome at
Rustica and they are usually turned loose in the music
room, the tool room or the tractor barn. Sometimes they
stick around long enough to gobble a couple of mice,
maybe shed once or twice and then move on.

Last year, Gary brought over 3 four- to five-footers
and I think I brought 3 from Mackie Lloyd's home on
Glenville Road. All are doing fine and what I've seen
over time has been good, complete sheds, a sign of a
healthy snake.

So as it came to pass, the other day Gary called again,
with a five-footer-plus and wondered if he could bring it
over. 'Sure, I'm home. Come ahead," I told him.

Within a half hour Gary was here, with his 'snake
carrying case,' a plastic 5-gallon bucket with a plastic
milk crate for a lid. As I prepared to open it up and take
a look Gary moved a little farther back with each move.

In the bucket was a beautiful black snake, rather
skinny, and very agitated. I guess the ride over wasn't
all the best and the bumpy ride and being out of his
element certainly didn't do his mood any good.

Normally a black snake is docile and easy to pick up.
So, without gloves I reached in and started to grab the
snake, just behind the jaws, gently, and lift it out of the
bucket.

STH

With lightning speed, the snake jerked its head away from my right hand and nailed my left index finger and thumb big time and locked on. The fangs dug in pretty deep and it hurt for sure. I had little control of the snake.

Quickly, I put a glove on my right hand and this time was able to lift the snake out and safely let it loose in the barn. Off it slithered to the shadows where it would be a little more comfortable in its own skin, so to say.

By this time I was bleeding pretty good, which I guess is a good thing to clear away any chance of infection. Gary was concerned, and I rinsed the two

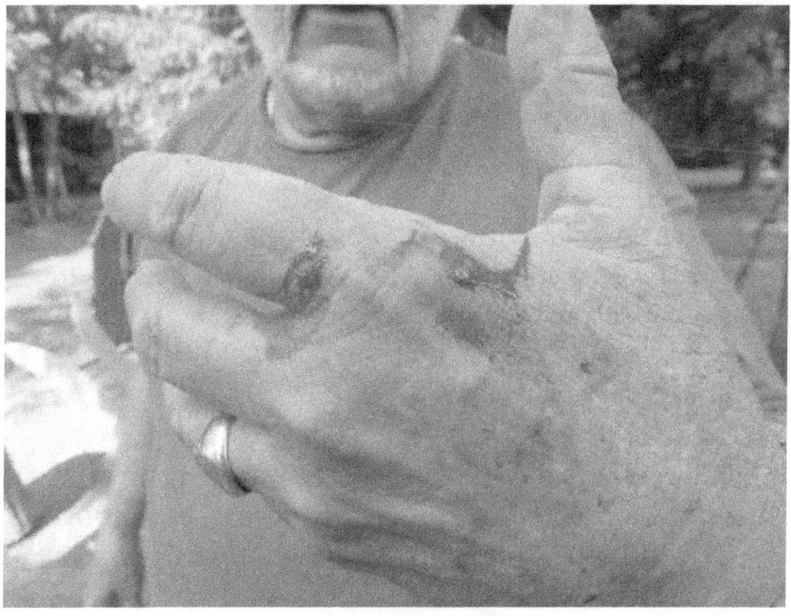

Woulda, coulda, shoulda...but, I didn't. Photo by Gary Rinehart.

Had it coming, I suppose. Photo by Gary Rinehart.

bites with cold water then some peroxide. Later I dosed
the bites with the Neosporin I always keep on hand and
bandaged them just to be on the safe side.

It was my own fault really. Maybe I should have just
carried the bucket up to the barn, laid it on its side and
let the snake come out on its own. It was my curiosity
as to the length that made me want to lift it out so that
could be determined.

In a recent article I gave advice on leaving creatures
where they are if possible. It is always the best thing to
do. As long as they aren't hurt, they'll find their own

STH

way back to surroundings that are comfortable. But
when someone doesn't like snakes or simply is afraid of
them, taking them somewhere safe is the best thing...
above all, please don't kill them.

Aside from the curse of forever being tied to evil
on account of a couple of folks eating an apple a long
time ago, snakes are rather uninterested in humans and
actually perform a great service in the food chain.

Snakes can devour a lot of rodents that otherwise
would overrun a home or garage. I have no problem
with turning them loose in the garage or close to the
house.

Nothing upsets me more than hearing that someone
beat a snake to death with a shovel or a hoe. It's also sad
to see a beautiful snake squished on the road.

Any wildlife deserves better than becoming
'roadkill'...but with all the traffic and normal routes the
wildlife take, it's bound to happen. The more we build
and grow and convert our woodlands to apartment
or new home dwellings, the more vigil we must be in
protecting the wildlife.

Just give wildlife a break...and whenever you can,
allow them to free-range. They won't stick around long;
they will forage for food and move on.

STH

Oh, just one other thing. When or if you do happen to handle a snake, use a bit of caution. I'm a pretty decent snake handler and on this occasion I plain forgot some of my own rules. I'm all healed up now and ready if Gary or Mackie gives me a call.

========= 30 =========

Bud Lloyd...A Remembrance On His 100th

S ome men are recognized for their kindness or gentle character. Some are revered for the good works or deeds they have done in their lifetimes. The accolades may be presented upon retirement from years of hard work or perhaps on a milestone of reaching 75 years of age and still going. It is nice to be recognized.

Then there are those who break all the rules. The adventure that is told here is the story of Bud Lloyd on the occasion of what would

1934

Bud Lloyd was a premier player in the Susquehanna League, playing first and third base for Havre de Grace. Photo from the Mac Lloyd Collection.

have been his 100th birthday year. Everything you will read here is true and when you are finished, see if you agree with the notion that here was a true Paul Bunyan of our local area. No matter, this is recognition worth sharing.

Bud Lloyd was born a man's man on May 15, 1911. He worked hard and played hard. Those who knew him say he could have used a little more discipline and a little less impulsiveness. Maybe so, but he was also fiercely competitive and hated the thought of losing anything...a ballgame...card game...anything. He was an outstanding baseball player known for his competitive fire and home run power.

He was also a generous man. He always took care of those who couldn't take care of themselves if he liked them. At the same time, he was a man of little patience. He suffered no fools and had no time for crooks or shysters. He lived his life on the square and by all accounts enjoyed that life.

Bud loved his family very much and he often said he was a 'very wealthy man' because of his family. His 'family' was his wife, Darcy, and children, Allen M., Beverly and Jo Beth Lloyd. Darcy recently celebrated her 94th birthday and still lives in the same home where she and Bud raised their family.

He took up golf in his late forties, won a Harford County Senior Tournament championship and First Flight championship at Pleasant Valley where he had two holes-in-one. Even though he was approaching senior status, young bucks at the golf course would want to be in his foursome because they knew they'd have a real good time.

STH

Bud was a handsome man. He bought his suits at
Griffith-Smith, a high dollar men's store in York, PA,
and they knew how to outfit him. He was also the life
of the party. His motto could have been 'too much of a
good thing is a good thing.' Folks would just gravitate
to him. He could seemingly go anywhere within 200
miles of Harford County and invariably he'd run across
somebody who knew him. And yes, as you might expect,
he could tell a good joke and tell it well.

He worked hard and lived hard like so many of his
generation and ilk, for that was the way of life. He was a
giver, not a taker. He was a joiner...Odd Fellows, Legion,
VFW, Masons, Shriners. He was content to be involved
in life no matter the challenge.

In honor of what would have been Bud Lloyd's 100th
Birthday, below are some facts and anecdotes that paint
the picture of this man's man.

****

Bud grew up poor. As a child, getting a box of
candy and an orange for Christmas was a big deal. One
Christmas morning, he proudly announced that he had a
present the whole family could use...a wash cloth.

****

STH

When Bud was a teenager, Whiteford grocer Hyman Reamer would routinely give him his new shoes to 'break in' and return. With his colorful and impulsive nature established early in life, Bud once chased down a dog that had bitten him and he proceeded to bite the dog.

****

Bud became one of the premier baseball players in the Susquehanna League, playing either first base or third base for Havre de Grace. Bud also played at different times for Perryville and Scarboro. After his Susquehanna League games, Bud would make an occasional appearance for the Port Deposit Blue Sox, an otherwise all-black team in a so-called black league. Bud was held in high regard by the black community in both Harford and Cecil counties. A noted slugger, Bud once hit three home runs in a big playoff game that gave Havre de Grace the pennant.

Bud's final blast sailed through the open door of a box car resting on the tracks beyond left field. The several thousand fans in attendance, who had reportedly bet a lot of money on the contest, were so ecstatic over Bud's heroics that they poked currency through the chicken-wire backstop. The batboy was sent to retrieve the money and returned with $250, which was a tidy sum in those days.

STH

Baseball contract from the Susquehanna League circa 1934. Contract negotiations and multi-million dollar agreements weren't even a thought in those times. Photo from the Mac Lloyd Collection

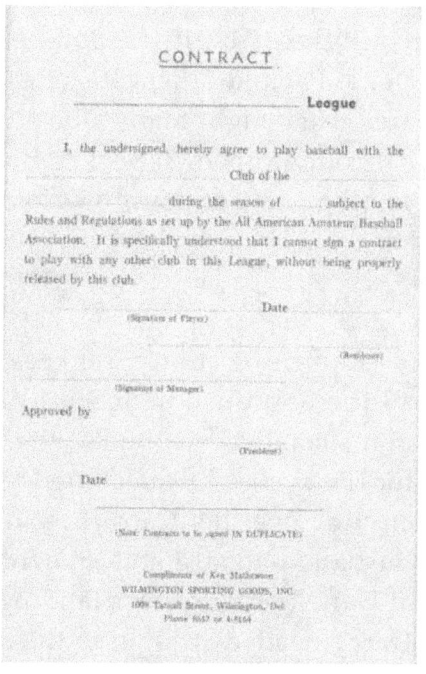

Oliver 'Big Rip' Ripken, a Susquehanna League player for rival Aberdeen, remembers Bud as being 'a bear of a ballplayer.' An editorial cartoon that appeared in a Havre de Grace newspaper depicted a hapless Susquehanna League third baseman with a gaping hole in his torso left by a smoking line drive off of Bud's bat under the heading 'Bud Hits A Sizzler.'

A Cecil County paper started one story by detailing how Bud was being given a constant ride by a heckler which eventually prompted Bud to dash from third base and into the crowd to punch his bedeviler right in the kisser. Bud later managed the Hickory team in the Susquehanna League where he signed a 15-year-old speedy outfielder named Dick Hall, who later pitched for the Orioles, to a contract after a brief workout.

In the early fifties, Bud helped John H. Beakes of
Delta, Pa. and others start Little League Baseball in the
area. He bought many a box of baseballs and a slew of
bats out of his own pocket. Bud would occasionally treat
small groups of boys to Orioles games.

****

Returning from a Yankees doubleheader in New York
a little past dusk with Scott Whiteford at the controls
of his small plane, Bud's wife, Darcy, who had retired
for the evening, was alerted to the sound of an airplane
circling over her Cardiff residence. Assuming it was her
husband onboard and knowing that there were no lights
at Dan Stewart's grass landing strip just north of town,
Darcy headed straight to the nearby Atlantic service
station and quickly recruited everybody there with a car
to come to the fliers' rescue. Within minutes, the cars
split up at the airfield, and with their headlights marking
the way, Scott was able to make a safe landing.

****

Prior to his death in 1979 at age 67, Bud had
established a ritual of delivering Thanksgiving and
Christmas dinners to a handful of widowers and
bachelors in the community, making sure they had a
good home cooked meal with all the trimmings directly
from Darcy's kitchen even before he sat down at his
family's table.

STH

****

When he sank his first hole-in-one, he was quoted in a local paper as saying he was so excited that he didn't know whether to laugh or cry. Darby Nace, a preacher at a Delta, Pa. church at the time, was an occasional Saturday golfer at Pleasant Valley. Like everyone else, he didn't have a caddy, but he did have strong moral support in Bud, who would utter a cuss word or two in the reverend's behalf whenever the clergyman hit an errant shot, which would elicit a 'thanks Bud' in return.

****

He was particular about his work, never cutting corners. A man working for him once told him he spent too much time on the finished product while plastering obscure places like clothes closets since hardly anyone would ever notice the flaws of a quick job. Bud's response was, "I'd know it wasn't done right." Between them, longtime friend Walter Moody of Dublin and Bud had four season tickets to Colts football games starting in 1958. They travelled to New York that season and witnessed the NFL championship match with the Giants in what was later dubbed 'The Greatest Game Ever Played.' Moody said that when Bud would stop by his market on his way from a hard day's work, Bud would be a rugged looking character with plaster splattered on his clothes and stuck to his ears and eyebrows. "But boy, when he got dressed up, I was proud to be seen with him."

STH

****

Although he wasn't a member of the local fire company, Bud would occasionally be called upon to help retrieve drowning victims from the watery slate quarries. Secured by a rope, Bud would be lowered over the jagged, rocky ledge and haul the deceased back to land draped over Bud's shoulder, a mission that required both strength and fearlessness.

Former Harford County High Sheriff Bill Kunkel remembers Bud and his talents. "Bud did all the plastering and stucco when I built my home on Watervale road in Fallston in 1962. Did a great job, first class."

Another pal and side-kick of Bud's was Jack Grafton, who now lives in Edgewood.

"I grew up in Delta, completing grades 2 through 10 at Slate Ridge High School in the 1940s. My earliest memory of Allen B. 'Bud' Lloyd is of him playing on the Delta-Cardiff baseball team at the Delta Community baseball diamond. I can still picture him playing first base, bent over, slapping his mitt, swinging his derriere, and daring the batter to hit one towards him.

"I remember Bud strolling after dinner a few doors down to the front of Dick Rees' poolroom where several men would gather, men like Hun Bennington, Bunny Watkins, Winder Williams, Duck Cantler, Toddy Lloyd,

Johnny Norris, Gwynne Holden, Rabbit Bennington, Bobby Watkins, Shinner Dooley, Clay Whiteford, John J. Roberts, Chippy Roberts...

"They would be discussing local and world events of the day. When Bud joined, the folks became listeners instead of talkers, because they were more interested in Bud's perspective and opinions on subjects of interest.

"Bud was a very sociable and personable man, until you crossed or challenged him. He was in the business of plastering ceilings and walls in new homes and one of his long-time employees was Kenny Cantler. They worked hard together and fought hard together. They were one of the most feared duos in the area when it came to fisticuffs.

"Midway Inn, just north of the Conowingo Dam, was owned and sometimes bar tended by Bill Webb. He told me of the hot afternoon when three buddies were already at the bar drinking when Bud and Kenny stopped for a cold one at the other end of the bar on their way home from work. Within a few minutes, the three began making disparaging remarks, loud enough for Bud and Kenny to hear, about them being a couple 'Delta Toughies' who 'think they're so bad!'

"Then two of them made the mistake of coming over to Bud and Kenny to make their remarks in a harassing way. Bill Webb told me that Bud and Kenny kept flooring the three of them until they became smart enough to remain on the floor, until 'The Delta Duo'

walked over slowly, drank up what remained in their
beer bottles, walked to Bud's green and white pick-up
and continued home.

"Bud was a man among men, hard working, athletic,
and proud of his military service to his country. In the
late 1940s, I believe most everyone in Delta, Cardiff and
Whiteford had heard of Bud Lloyd and liked him if they
knew him."

****

Delta's Thomas Louis 'Kenkaid' Scotten remembers
Bud when he was a Little League coach. Ken played for
Bud, as a starting pitcher, with a mean curve ball.

"I'll never forget, as a kid, before I played baseball,
we were at the Delta diamond and Bud was playing in a
'pick-up' game. He took his bat and pointed it at a field
light atop a telephone pole in left field. Just like Babe
Ruth did, Bud did the exact same thing. Then he hit the
ball right at the light and busted it into little pieces. I'll
never forget that sight as long as I live.

"Then and there I wanted to play baseball for Bud
Lloyd. He was impressive. He was the best, ever. In
school I was on the 'safety patrol' and all of us got to
go to Philadelphia to see a professional baseball game.
Willie Mays hit two home runs that day, and from then
on I wanted to play baseball. Bud Lloyd and Willie Mays
stick in my mind as inspirations to play ball."

****

Allen B. 'Bud' Lloyd was a great man. There are many great men who never flew solo across the Atlantic, occupied the White House, or who had a lot of power. These men are heroes to us not for any great deed or any one accomplishment. Men like Bud Lloyd are the heroes in our lives who we can learn from, appreciate how they've lived, and remember with respect. I never really 'knew' Bud Lloyd, but my grandmother Addie Holden sure did. I remember being with her at the Delta Telephone Exchange late at night and her getting a call from Bud...he would start out, "Aunt Addie, I need a favor..." She would help him out, and that was that. She, like so many others in Delta, loved the man. I truly wish I had known him better, although knowing of him and hearing all the stories and adventures, I'm glad I got this close.

========= 30 =========

Author's note...I would like to thank all those who contributed to this article, especially Tyler Lloyd, a grandson of Bud Lloyd, who suggested writing the article.

This is an official doodle page. Feel free to jot down
your grocery list, notes to self, or just scribble away.

*   *   *

Bel Air's Roller Rink
A Landmark For The Ages

Pictured in 2005, the building is more than 50 years old.
Surrounded by stores and houses today, when it was built in the
early 1950s it stood alone. Photo by Todd Holden.

Just give anyone directions around Bel Air and nine
times out of ten you'll use the famed Bel Air Roller Rink
as a point of location. "Just up old Route 1 past the roller
rink and left on ..." You get the idea.

Built in 1952, the skating rink was purely a "Delta
(Pennsylvania) Project" and to this day the engineering
still baffles and amazes engineers, contractors and
architects. You see, when the suits all said it couldn't
be done: a single span, 100-foot truss without center
support poles, Mr. Joseph "Bumps" Orr said it could and
he did it. This is the Delta way. Just ask anyone born
and raised there. The ingenuity and resourcefulness
from that little borough across the border is legendary.
Whether it's a green marble quarry or a slate clock,
Delta's been there and done that.

STH

When Bumps ran his little grocery store in downtown Highland, just five miles down the road from Delta, nights were spent figuring out how to build a large skating rink with no poles to interfere with the skaters. With his savvy and some of Charley Durham's cash the two men sought out Marshall Scarborough and his son, who were Delta contractors. To the amazement of locals, the 100-foot wooden "bow-string" trusses were lowered into place with a small crane a few months later.

Mr. Scarborough considered himself a carpenter. He spent years building wooden trusses at the Aberdeen Proving Ground as well as Edgewood Arsenal during wartime. While learning the craft he had the good fortune to meet an engineer who helped him with books and strategy. Soon the Scarboroughs were on their own and gathering even more information from timber engineers in Washington.

Each of their trusses contains 2,501 feet of lumber. At the time of construction the limit for wood trusses was 120 feet. The greatest advantage of wood in 1951 was that it was cheaper than steel. The Scarboroughs could make one truss a day with their crew. They used a long, perfectly level platform, and laid out the pattern. The bowstring across the top was formed by a series of 2X4's bent, glued and bolted in the "vise-stabilized pattern," according to a news item in a local paper at the time.

STH

Then the rest of the truss is laid into place and all attaching holes are bored and marked. Between each joint, at every bolt, a ring four inches around is countersunk, giving the joint as much strength as a solid plank, the article stated.

The frames were disassembled after each job and transported to the next site where wooden trusses were required for large construction projects.

In an interview, Ms. Hagy mentions the roof trusses being built by a company in the Whiteford area. A little post-interview investigation determined that the trusses were built on-site by R. Marshall and W. Robert Scarborough (father and son, Scarborough Builders, Inc.) of Delta, PA. A 1953 Aegis article contained significant coverage of the construction, as these trusses were the longest span in any building on the east coast and was only exceeded by one other building in the U.S. (somewhere on the west coast). Photo from the Carol DeRan Collection.

STH

"The key to the truss," according to Mr. Scarbourgh, "was the runner on the lower side of the frame being built with a very slight arc. This will never settle into a straight position, making it a powerful truss."

And so it came to be. The big rink opened and withstood the Blizzard of '59, with its ice pack, heavy snows and power outages. They said it couldn't be done, and Delta did it. Plain and simple. And it remained open, albeit on a more limited scale than in its heyday.

A faded cardboard sign on the entrance reads, "Closing 6/16/99----Re-Open 9/10/99. Have a Great Summer. See you In September."

Soon after opening in 1952, the Orrs and Mr. Durham raised hundreds of dollars for the Heart Fund through benefits at the skating rink from 1952 to 1968. Sadly, in 1997 Mrs. Catherine Orr died of heart disease. Bumps sold out his interest to Charley in 1968. Bumps died November 11,1995, and Charley died in 1996. An acquaintance of Mr. Durham, Ms. Eloise Hagy, is now running the show.

Today, Bumps' stepdaughter, Carol DeRan, helps oversee three other skating rinks in and around Raleigh, North Carolina. She has no say in the Bel Air rink.

She recalls the Buddy Deane 'sock hops' held at the rink during the early '50s and some of the rock and roll stars that came with the sometimes-tottering Deane, who was known to reek of the nectar when he visited Bel Air.

STH

If you do not own your own skates, they are available for rental.
Photo from the Carol DeRan Collection.

"We had to empty out the rink at 10:30 in the evening and then the sock hop fans paid $2 each to get in to hear the music. We split the take with Buddy, who watched the gate personally," said Carol. A good evening of dancing teenagers yielded good returns for the Orrs at a time when money had more mojo.

With crowds of 1000, standing room only and rock blasting, cars were parking along both sides of Route 1, in fields and anywhere else they could. Buddy Deane hops were the most happening thing in the county. Life and the times were good.

A visit to the rink recently revealed only road crews working on the extended by-pass, that will now pass through my deceased Uncle Sabret Richardson's old

STH

home place, which adjoins the former Orr property. Word had it long ago that Sabe stopped the road construction right at the roller rink, and it stayed that way for many years. Sabe was a farmer and "no state government was gonna take my place away or run a road through it." And until now, and tens of thousands more people, did it happen.

And so the landmark stands, freshly painted, withstanding hurricanes, ice storms, blizzards and sporadic snowstorms. And the folks like Roland Streett, Sammy Orr and Carol DeRan will forever hold powerful memories of skating to organ music on a shiny cushioned floor, and the memorable announcement, "Couples Only."

========= 30 =========

Note: Repeated attempts to contact the current owner Eloise Hagy were fruitless.

Todd Holden writes from his home, Rustica. He never learned how to skate backwards like Sammy Orr or Roland Streett.

Ready and Waitin'

W as a time when things were smoother in
Hickory. Brownie's Log Cabin was a good
place to go on Sunday for a fine dinner. Cappy's was a
good place for a little crab cake and a beer.

Bill Gibson ran the service station catty-corner from
Cappy's...he was the best friend any teenager could have
to keep their car on the go. He sold gas and repaired all
makes and models. He would come out on a rainy night
and tow out your dad's Buick Roadmaster from a dirt
lane off Thomas Run road.

Those days are gone for good. Sadly, time and
progress have taken their toll in the little speck on Route
1 known as Hickory. In its day Hickory was smack on
that major highway, seeing hundreds of cars a day pass
by, with folks stopping in to buy gas, food, lodging or
a little crab cake from Cappy's. It was the same road
that linked Maine to Florida and passed right through
Hickory and Bel Air.

A favorite business of mine was John M. Spicer's
farm equipment store in downtown Hickory. John was
a unique businessman. A good man, self-made if you
will. And he made some others successful as well. John
and his wife, Eula, had four sons...the oldest and the
youngest were the ones who stuck with the business and

STH

Thomas Edward Spicer (left) and Samuel Morgan Spicer in 1988 at their father's farm equipment store in Hickory. Photo by Todd Holden.

did most of the work. That would be Samuel Morgan Spicer, the elder, and Thomas Edward Spicer, the youngest. They are the two dudes in the above photo.

Those two men could fix anything...they could make a box of Cracker Jacks run...they just had the natural talent to fix all mechanical things. From a large tractor or combine, or hay rake...they could find the parts, install them, and you were back in the fields bringing in the sheaves, so to speak. Farmers constantly battled changing weather, like rain on fresh cut hay, and equipment failures. The Spicer's could remedy only one, and they did so with speed, economy and satisfaction.

STH

As time went on the boys got into selling Triumph Motorcycles, at that time bringing the second oldest son, John Robert 'Saus' Spicer into the business. Bob was good at one thing, making anything go faster...including his red '57 Chevy, or a Triumph Trident motorcycle.

Those were the good days whenever a trip to 'Spicer's' was in order. They were good, innocent times when you could walk in and see one or two friends who were there either to shoot the breeze or get parts for something that was broken. You could learn a lot just listening to some of the old timers. You could also ask a question and not get a 'sales pitch' but an honest answer.

Tommy and Sam sold me one of the first riding lawnmowers in the county, a Massey-Ferguson 7 horsepower rig, with a 36-inch mower deck that was the cat's whiskers at the time. It lasted a long time, with Tommy putting in a new engine after 15 years of mowing. When it was near the end of the mowing days, Tommy's son, Brian Thomas, sold me a Wheel Horse, 12 horsepower, with a 42-inch, rear-discharge deck in 1984 and I mowed with it yesterday. Still has the original engine and Earl McIntire keeps it on the go now.

Longevity...hard to come by today, even when we care for our mowers and tractors and motorcycles. The thing is, I miss places where you could stop in with no particular problems and absorb stuff that was interesting and helpful, if ever you did have a problem. The store long ago closed up. Tommy died way too soon, and Sam

got into huge satellite dishes way before I had ever seen
or heard of one. I still stay in touch with Sam, even if
it's not in the old garage where we first met.

He is one of the smartest persons I know. He's good
at everything he does...whether it's a game of chess,
playing the banjo or turning an 11.5 seconds quarter mile
in his 2002 Camaro SS at the drags. It is 'Street Legal
Performance'....Sam wouldn't have it any other way.
I've known him most of my life, one of the best pals ever.
I've ridden with him when he raced Norm Stinchcomb
on 'Spicer's Flats' north of Hickory at Mount Tabor
Church in his '55 Chevy.

Tommy's widow continued at the old store with
her sewing and fabric business, now it's gone as well.
But when I pass by the old store, it's still the same to
me. The new by-pass kinda quieted down the traffic on
that stretch of road...in the name of progress, but that's
not a bad thing...it's just slower paced...with some fine
businesses still flourishing.

Missing is Cappy Williams' crab cakes; Bill Brown's
antique shop; Bill Gibson's tow truck and John Swamm,
his mechanic; Phillips T.V.; Bob Farrington's Mobile
station; and Spicer's. Little bits of Americana that were
such a big part of a lot of lives for a long time. And like
the box turtle and pheasants, they are gone, never to be
back again...but a treasure while they were with us.

========= 30 =========

He Is Good To Me

S he was a great traveling pal, all the way across the country, the two of us and a cooler full of water, raisins, nuts, beer and chardonnay. We had such a great time...four weeks on the road, never a cross word or argument, even though I nearly ran out of gas twice and we both were stranded atop Rollins Pass in Colorado without water and were fast dehydrating.

Lots of laughter was the norm, as she 'ran the bank' with money for food that we pooled when we left town. After two or three days, it's like we were made to travel the roads of this country and find out what was out there, in places we'd never been. Road trips are like that...adventures into the unknown, and learning things about what we've known in the past.

We met again for the first time at a class reunion meeting and began a four-year relationship that was beautiful. Both divorced with children that thought we were made for each other...everyone thought that except me...and I was afraid of failing to be what she wanted me to be....when it was good it was great, when it wasn't so good, it was lonely and brought back old memories of a previous time.

STH

I Can't Get You Off Of My Mind

Old habits are hard to break, matters of the heart are never the same for any of us...like minded maybe, same ages or close to, backgrounds may vary yet the heart levels the playing field...and play we do...new leaves on the tree, greener grass often tempts the weak among us. Some, like the Canada's that fly northward, are mated for life, such is the case for many of us. Dalliances come and go, some more than others, never seemed to be rewarding for me.

Seems like the deeper the love for someone, the harder and longer it takes to move on as the preachers and shrinks advise. The loves we have shared don't come back to haunt us, more to remind us of what we learned from that person...not what we regret.

Others fill the gaps making life bearable...friends, children, maybe a relative or two, in each unique way, there is something to offer, to appreciate, and to welcome into the heart.

It's just so hard to start all over again, when it comes to love, a companion and a new set of 'family' to add to the old one. I'm just not up to it...if you are, you are lucky, and I wish you the best. Sometimes we run into 'solo livers' in the grocery store...and we exchange news of what we've been up to....and it's all good, to share and share alike.

STH

Sometimes one of our pals enters a 'serious relationship' with someone else who is alone...not talking here about deceit and deception and cutting out on a spouse or live-in...no treason.

Speaking of two folks, men, women, young and old, who 'find each other' in one way or the other...and stroll into the sunset. It happens but it's rare...when it does, and works out, with neither of the two giving more than '50%'...then it's a deal made in Heaven. I've never thought much of e-Harmony.com...and other services that match up folks...who knows, it might be fine for others... just not for me.

And so it was my old pal, who moved on and moved from Maryland to North Carolina, is happy in her new home on the golf course...she plays a helluva round of golf...straight up, and no 'monkey business'...she's met a pal, she writes me and says it's all good..."He is good to me, treats me nice," she wrote....and it's all that simple...someone romping into their 70s and still golfing, traveling and enjoying life is lucky to be with someone.

"But," she adds, "it's not the same as when we were together...we had it all, and it just didn't work out." No blame, no shame, no guilt...just two folks who were strong willed and held to their beliefs...and there's nothing wrong with that. Maybe it makes us stronger, because we remain true to ourselves.

STH

Maybe none of this would have happened if luck
would have prevailed. But I'm glad it did and I'm more
fulfilled inside than if we hadn't gotten together, hadn't
settled in to finding out about each other, hadn't taken
that ride across the country. What's even a warmer
feeling is that she feels the same, enriched by our paths
crossing. It's all good.

========= 30 =========

Some Folks Never Say 'I'm Sorry'

A pal sent me an e-mail the other day and mentioned a visitor had stopped by his house. The visitor happened to be a mutual acquaintance of ours and I replied, asking how the person was. The response came back, 'Not bad. Fragile, philosophical... calm.' I knew my pal to be accurate with his words, so I knew they were genuine.

After reading those succinct words of description my only thought was..."The man who never said, 'I'm sorry'." I certainly wish no ill will and don't feel happy for anyone being fragile. Actually, I shake my head and understand that in a certain way, a toll has been exacted. It's just how I feel and it applies to a couple friends of mine and maybe a relative or two. Consideration for others should be a big part of our lives and when that kindness isn't there and saying sorry never comes to pass, it's just sad. Sooner or later, it'll come back to haunt you.

We all make mistakes, some days more than others, some folks more than others, then we realize our misstep and commit to saying we're sorry to whomever we might have offended. Sometimes it takes a little spunk to muster the words, at least for some people, but never for me...I've said it probably too often, just out of guilt that I may have inadvertently hurt someone's feelings.

STH

It's not such a hard thing to do, this saying "I'm sorry."

Yet there are those who I've never heard those words from, it's as if they'd choke if they said them. On one hand, I feel sympathy for them and hope they can come to terms with their behavior. Yet, there comes a time when 'enough is enough' and I feel like they never will learn those words. Too bad, because some of those people I've had to cut loose.

Sure, I asked how the fella was doing, and the reply came back 'fragile, philosophical...calm.' I inquired how they were doing because I still care, and think of the individual, sort of 'just checking in'....but that's it, no more, no less. When I replied, "the man who never said, 'I'm sorry'," the response was a sighful, 'I know, I know.'

So it goes without saying, we maybe aren't close friends anymore. Sometimes we grow apart, in philosophies or space and distance, but we don't forget friends. Perhaps some of my Scots-Irish blood compels it, but how I've lived also speaks to compassion being a big part of my life. Others understand this. We get our feelings hurt just like everyone else. Most times one or the other makes the first move and things get patched up and life goes on.

But when it's always the same one doing the apologizing, it gets old. Then, we get back on our heels and begin to feel differently. Where there was sympathy there is now resentment. Ultimately, we realize that we

STH

cannot lose our own self-respect at the expense of saving a relationship, no matter how deep or what the cost is to our emotions.

Self-respect and the way we try to live our lives, especially in these times, is foremost for many of us. To live our lives on the square and strive to show kindness to others is what it's about. To live differently is self-destructive and unhealthy. If we didn't have values then why would that person who never says 'I'm sorry' even want to be our friend in the first place?

So, we look in the mirror every morning and think about what the day might bring. We have a clear conscience, and those who we speak to we speak honestly and listen with empathy. The give and take of life becomes good.

When we speak with that person who just doesn't get it, who never learned compassion or saying sorry, we are uncomfortable as the conversation develops. Differences of opinion become disparate individuals and out of deference, we hold our tongue, although we really want to let them have it. Yet, hostility is not the way to live, and at the expense of causing a problem, we acquiesce and let things slide. Again, the man who never says, 'I'm sorry,' can continue being who he is. Perhaps he or she gains momentum when they are in a situation where they know they should and refuse to say they're 'sorry.'

STH

There comes a time when our confidence grows and we embrace that self-respect we have cultured. We know in our heart of hearts that our honesty must guide us. Tolerance of people is one thing, but tolerating ill behavior is quite another. Then with confidence in ourselves at a particular time, that individual happens to trigger that gut feeling we all know of...only this time, we say what's in our hearts...

It might be us saying, 'I'm sorry.' Maybe this time we've done nothing to say those precious words for, and once in a while we just bring the wagons to a halt and say our piece and let the chips fall where they may...

Here's the chance for the other person to make it right, or at least try to make it right...and they don't... They are just that stuck in their own self-importance they won't do it.

That's a shame but it's just the way things are sometimes. Some folks are pretty stubborn, even if we are the ones who apologize first. They are hard-core, and I can't tell you why...they just are. And so, we think of these persons every now and then. When their names come up in thought or conversation we think of the good times for a few minutes, then we move on, because we tried to mend the fences, as we always have, and we just got tired of trying.

========= 30 =========

She Listened With Her Eyes

There are people we know who really are part of the fabric of our own lives. A son or daughter, a close relative, or a friend who you just can't live without...they all touch us in ways to complete our time on this earth.

Imagine also the people we've met who we barely know. Every now and then it's a real shocker to read the obituaries and see a name of someone you've known for a long time...not so much as a friend, even though most of them are, but someone who you have crossed paths with and casually known.

Maybe it was someone in a retail business you may have frequented through the years. Or someone who you ran into on your errands through town and something magical happens as a friendship opens up. There is an exchange of glances or a nod and perhaps that's all that's needed.

The amazing thing is that while the friendship begins and ends there for the most part, it can easily be a friendship every bit as strong as the ones with our close friends and family. Deloris Walters was one such friendship.

STH

"Deloris M. Walters, age 78, of Bel
Air, MD passed away suddenly
on September 18, 2011 at Upper
Chesapeake Medical Center in Bel
Air, MD. Born in Bristol, VA, she was
the daughter of the late Lawrence
Huston and Nina Gladys Miller Large.

She worked as an optician for many
years and enjoyed gardening at
the age of 78 where she still used
her own chainsaw to cut up trees.
She was always doing for others."

The lady I knew only as Deloris was the oldest of
eight children, born in Bristol, Virginia. I met her when
she worked for Bel Air Opticians, then located at the
corner of Main and Lee streets in Bel Air. The glasses
that I had worn since I was about 6 years old were very
tight, plastic frames that gave me many a headache. The
optician before Bel Air Opticians came along had told
me that because I had such a small nose the frames and
'temples' had to be tight to keep the glasses on my head.

I accepted that and the pain those glasses gave me,
all through Saint Margaret and Bel Air High School, and
college. Then one day Quincy Edwards told me about a
new optician in Bel Air, Earl Cross, and I might want to
check his store out.

I did, and met both Earl and Deloris...and from that
day on, my life and vision changed forever.

They asked me that day if I liked the music of the Beatles, and John Lennon. I said I sure did...and Deloris came out of the back room with a pair just like Lennon wore.

I was blown away. The frames they offered me were wire-rimmed, gold filled and felt like they weren't even on my face. No more headaches and no more little grooves along my sideburns.

Deloris and I became good friends and when her daughter, Deborah, got married she asked me to shoot it.

Deborah told me a few years ago her mom was using a chain saw to cut up limbs and sustained a severe cut on her forearm. "The surgeons who sewed it up said she could have lost her arm that day. She was 72 at the time and my brother and I managed to get the chain saw away from her to avoid a future accident. Wouldn't you know, Delores went right out and bought another one," Deborah said.

On September 17th, Dee woke up with 'a horrifying headache' and Alan immediately called 911. She was taken to Upper Chesapeake Hospital and died the following day. Her family believes it could have been a severe stroke. She was not put on 'life support'...the family stating she would never want to live like that, without being active any more.

STH

Over the years I would run into Deloris at a store,
a restaurant or the doctor's office. The last time I saw
her and her husband Alan Edelstein was at Dr. Joseph
Reinhardt's office and as usual she had a lot to talk about
and fill me in on. She lived near Bel Air, and yes, she
operated her own chain saw at the age of 78...but she sure
didn't look or act like a 78 year old.

There are many people we meet and like in the 'retail
trade' or in the doctor's offices where we run into one
another. These are people we 'connect' with, just for
those occasions when we have an appointment. We don't
see them in church, or socially, just on 'business terms'...
and we never forget them.

She was a fun person to know and we got along great.
She certainly made my vision so much better with her
talents in the optical shop. She could listen with her eyes
and understand. She was the kind of person I wanted
to be when it came to me dealing with my customers...I
learned many lessons of service in retail from her.

I also learned the fun of practical jokes from Dee, like
the time she and Earl soldered a quarter to a nail and
put it into a spacer on the Main street sidewalk outside
their store window. She called me at the newspaper and
said she had an idea for some fun pictures. I went over
and set up my camera inside the store and caught several
people, young and old, trying to pick up that quarter and
failing.

STH

It was April 1st...a very special day to Dee and me as well. It was harmless fun, and she was surely a lady who could take it and dish it out. She was one of a kind and I'll never forget her.

She 'went out the way she wanted to go' her daughter said at Deloris' eulogy. Days before she died she was working cleaning up the aftermath of hurricane Irene. One lady suggested they put the chain saw in the casket with Deloris, or 'Dee' as most folks called her. Instead roses were placed in the casket.

There are special places and special faces in our life and times. Images that don't fade with time, then one day, they are gone. The drum is banged yet again and we continue on.

========= 30 =========

Don't forget to hug your mother.
Think fast if she's holdin' a chainsaw or packin'.

*   *   *

The Days Of
Local Racing Teams

I n addition to all the wedding and portrait shots, there were pictures of special events I attended, 'in the right place at the right time' shots, and sometimes just me and the 35mm Leica M-3 out on the road. The sheer volume of my photographs and father time smiling kindly on me sort of dictate that I can't remember every face or subject. By far, the most passionate moments were off the cuff, gather-round shots I made of friends and strangers living life simply and being proud with their own passions.

A simple inquiry about a photograph I had made in 1967 at the Jarrettsville Service Center of a bunch of guys and a beautiful race car sparked a challenge to identify those in the picture. An added bonus to the shot can be seen peeking out from between the second and third guys standing by the race car. She is Daria McDaniel.

A question from the wife of one of the men in the shot, Mrs. Pat Gross, who asked who the people were in this classic photograph from days long ago prompted me to find out for myself who these men were and how the racing team came to be.

I began by asking several friends if they might know anything about such a 'racing team'...one thing led to another and former Harford County Sheriff Bill Kunkel,

STH

who rarely steers me wrong, said a retired deputy, Dave Saneman, might know something, as well as Rodney Peak, who operates a machine shop in Jarrettsville.

Sure enough, from the hot tip, I made a few more inquiries and the names of the 'racing team' came my way. In the interest of racing fans still around and for those who can still remember the simpler life, here's the picture and the story behind it.

Left to right back row—Larry Johnson, Richard Boring, Marvin Carr, Stephen Saneman and Andy Moore. Kneeling front row-Harvey Gross, Jimmy Everett, Daniel Everett and George Gast. In between Boring and Carr, is the mascot of the car, Charlie McDaniel's daughter, Little Daria. Photo by Todd Holden, 1967.

STH

The real treat was getting in touch with David Saneman. Yes, he retired from deputy duties many years ago, but he still has a knack for the details.

"Around 1963-1964, a group of guys from Jarrettsville got together and decided to build a race car. We were all involved in drag racing. My twin brother, Steve, and I had a '56 Chevy with a 6 cyl. race engine we ran at York U.S. 30 Dragway and Cecil County Dragway. There were at least 10-12 guys including those in your picture that formed another team in 1978.

We collected dues and sponsored a New Years' Dance every year for 6-8 years.

Many of us during this time acquired muscle cars and street drag racing was the thing to do on weekends. Andy Moore had a Mercury Comet, Steve had a Dodge Coronet, and later, a Charger. Harvey Gross had a Mustang Cobra GT 500. We all hung out at the Jarrettsville Service Station on weekends.

We had a drag strip that we marked off beginning at the bridge over Morse Rd. heading toward Jarrettsville on New Rt 23.

MSP Trooper Otis Trost was very familiar with all of us and many times would make attempts to apprehend us for drag racing. He was a great guy, just doing his job.

STH

The racing team worked on the '39 Ford in the back lower side of the Blue Bell in the day. We also began building a 1932 five-window Ford Coupe, but we never finished it. Marvin drove the stock car at Grandview Race Track in Reading, Pennsylvania. We all worked as the pit crew. Dick Boring was the brains.

He knew engines and race setup inside and out. Dick and Bob Boring used to build engines for McCoy Racing back in the 1950s. The race car was destroyed in a traffic accident on the way to the race track one evening. Fortunately, no one was injured. It seems all of us eventually got married and raised families, leaving the racing to fade away. They were good times.

Harvey Gross, Marvin Carr, and Dick and Bob Boring have all passed away. My brother Steve remembers the little girl's name. She was Charles McDaniel's daughter. Charles ran the grocery store in Coopstown, not Jimmy McDaniel. The little girl's name was Daria. The name on the back of the race car is 'Little Daria.'

I forgot to mention, I had a 1965 GTO back then and I still have it."

David Saneman
Morse Road, Forest Hill, Md.

STH

Mackie Lloyd comments..."Pat was married to Harvey Gross (kneeling in first row, first one on left in pic). Harvey died last March in St. Andrew's, S.C., when he crashed his small plane while practicing touch-and-goes. They had moved south several years ago after living in Jarrettsville their entire lives. I don't know Pat's maiden name. She's a librarian at a public library.

Harvey and I were longtime pals. Went through basic training at Fort Jackson, spent 6 years in the National Guard, and went to countless car races together.

* * *

There you have it, an old photograph, bringing back many memories...thanks to Rodney Peak, Bill Kunkel, Dave Saneman and Mackie Lloyd. What a wonderful time it was back then in a time of fun loving innocence and adventure. The excitement for me is as much of a blast now as the day I took the photograph. Just being part of something so innocent and real is, well, about as real as it gets.

Another interesting part of this story, Andy Moore's son, Charlie Moore, is currently the Barrack Commander, Maryland State Police, at Benson. Otis Trost is alive and well, and has stories to tell, maybe in a later edition of the great days of Harford's past.

STH

From the lady who made this adventure possible, Pat Gross, comes this note:

"Thank you so much - Our children are going to be so excited!! Todd, your photo will be a prized possession in our family for many years to come! Thanks again and have a good day." - Pat Gross

========= 30 =========

Riding The 'Ma and Pa' To Delta

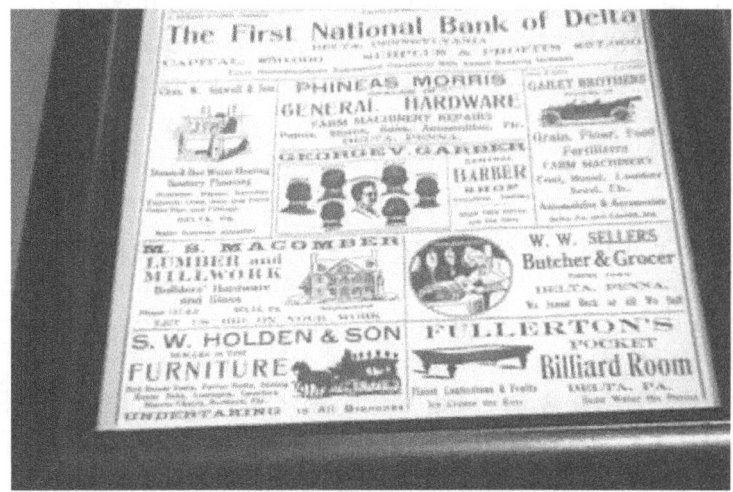

P eople that know me, know I can tell them local history every bit as accurate as the local book writers and with a sense of detail down to the names, nicknames, how folks lived and what they ate for their last meal. I've always been blessed with a good memory...part of that is being fascinated by the world around me from the time I was just a small boy. I paid attention and enjoy the memories.

There have been various books written about the 'Ma and Pa' railroad and I have enjoyed reading them. I've written about the problems up at Scott Creek along Bunker Hill Road north of Delta where the railroad meandered through. But I guess the richest rewards of this local railroad are the memories I have growing up and riding them.

For many years on Fridays my dad would take me to
the Bel Air station of the Maryland and Pennsylvania
railroad located at the north end of Bel Air, next to the
Southern States and Walters' Mills. The station itself
was a classic of architecture, and there were folks who
actually lived on the second floor of the station.

Most impressive was the big red, yellow and green
luggage wagon always parked next to the loading ramp.
All I had with me in those days was a leather satchel and
my bicycle. When dad bought my ticket, I always had a
choice of getting off in Whiteford, the longest bike ride
if the weather was good, or Cardiff, the closest, or the
Delta station, next to the fascinating slaughter house.

Outside the Ma and Pa station at the north end of Bel Air. This
photograph is from the collection of photographs in the recently
published *'The Ma & Pa Remembered, A History of the Maryland &
Pennsylvania Railroad,'* by Henry C. Peden Jr. and Jack L. Shagena Jr.

STH

Usually, I got off at the Cardiff stop, next to Jess Kohlbus' Mobile station and Robinson Brothers International-Harvester buildings, where I could check out the shiny red tractors and the model tractors they sold at Christmastime.

The ride to Delta in those days was by a car like the one pictured here. It pulled another car, usually a baggage car, where my bike rode. There were regular glass windows on this car and they shook when the train went over the Gross trestle at Sharon.

My trips to Delta in those days were twofold. First to visit my grandmother Addie Holden, who was widowed. I would help her around the house with chores, yard work and go to Slate Ridge Presbyterian Church with her on Sundays, where Mervyn Thompson was my Sunday School teacher.

Another reason for the train ride to Delta was piano lessons with Miss Enid Lewis at the east end of town where she lived with her brother, Ed. Miss Lewis was a fine lady, I loved her and the gentile way she put up with my labored lessons since I didn't do a lot of practicing during the week.

I did learn to play the piano though, and she even taught me to play an 'Arthur Godfrey Ukulele' my folks had given me. One night as I was roller skating back to Grandmother's with the lesson book and ukulele I got snagged on an up-heaved piece of the slate sidewalk and took a bad spill.

STH

Busted up my knee when I hit the edge of the slate
and the ukulele was in pieces. So ended my uke lessons.
It was dark that night and I couldn't find all the pieces of
the little instrument. I went back the next day with Lane
Hall and we found what was left of it. Even tried Testor's
model airplane glue to put it back together.

Actually, the slate sidewalks were fun to skate on in
the daytime, darting up and over the uneven places, kind
of like a steel-wheeled skate slalom.

After church and a great lunch at Jones' Restaurant
across from Robinson Brothers, we walked back to
grandmother's house behind the telephone exchange
and I had to pack up and get ready for the train ride
back home. It was sad to leave Delta and Lane and
head home, because that meant back to school and more
practice on the piano.

I would kiss my Grandmother Holden goodbye, get
on my bike and head for the Delta station, where the
train stopped on the one run on Sundays. The man took
my bike, loaded it up, and the conductor hollered out,
'All aboard'...and it was another great train ride home on
the most fun transportation an 11-year old could have.

========= 30 =========

'51 Hudson Still Ahead Of Its Time

[Editor's Note: This story was originally written in 1998, with the author admiring both the Hudson and the man. Sadly, Mr. Garrett passed away Friday, August 12, 2012. He was 76 years old and the husband of Mary F. Leftwich for 11 years. The author would like to share this story out of respect.]

Lowell Garrett admires his '51 Hudson. Photo by Todd Holden.

Some folks are born laid back. Some get calmer with age. Some never do settle down and act right. Lowell Ray Garrett was born mellow, with a wrench in his hand and fixing things on the farm before he could walk. Laid back was his style, although nobody knew the term in 1936.

STH

His home near Poplar Grove is where his cars rest, waiting for new engines, a paint job or reupholstery. The original '49 Chevy two-ton truck that he hauled scrap metal on when he was sixteen and still at North Harford High School is there.

"I hauled to the yards in Baltimore and brought back a load of gravel for the farm on the return trip," he said. "At one time or other I probably had 75 junked cars that I was working with or hauling away."

Raised on a farm, Lowell and his older brother Bill did all the chores while their dad worked at the Proving Ground in Aberdeen. In 1954, his senior year in high school, he drove a school bus and was well on his way to becoming an excellent mechanic. Even with this natural gift, Lowell wanted to work away from the farm near Prospect Road on Route 136. "I tried to get work at Martin's (Glenn L. Martin Co.) and Bendix, but they didn't want anything to do with me because I had diabetes. As soon as I told them that, they said, in so many words, they didn't need me."

"Bobby Gallion and I went to apply and Bobby was hired and wound up in California. I wound up back on the farm, so I just made the best of it," he acknowledges.

After the farm was sold in 1961, Lowell went to work for Harford County and then for 20 years made things purr at Plaza Ford. All during this time he worked with his brother, Bill, building a hugely successful Harley-Davidson dealership nearby. Now retired from active

STH

work and managing his diabetes with double shots of insulin and cocktails, he is content with his cars, especially the '51 Hudson two-door sedan he is about to put a 308 cubic inch Hornet engine in. "It will give it more power and make it a little snappy," Lowell says.

His first vehicles were trucks, naturally, and then came a 1951 Chevrolet four-door sedan. "Then I got interested in Hudson's. They were low down, streamlined and different and there weren't a lot of them. There were two Hudson dealerships in the county then. One in Darlington and one in Poplar Grove, operated by Jennings Scarborough, at the corner of Routes 1 and 136, where Harford Tire stands today.

The '51 Hudson looks like it's been chopped and channeled, but that's the way it was designed originally. In 1951, the engineers at Hudson All Steel Monobilt Body were seeing smooth, flowing lines, uncluttered by chrome and steel. The machines they made were downright sexy and they still have an alluring look today.

The windows are like slits in beady eyes, all around the car, and the fender skirts log in at just four inches high, that's how low the wheel wells come down around the tires. Inside there is plenty of head room, even though the appearance outside is one of 'low slung comfort.'

STH

A glove box big enough to hold a briefcase beckons beneath a maroon leather-covered dashboard. The speedometer goes to 110, possibly to 120. "I've only had it up to 80, I guess," Lowell admits. "I was lucky, years ago never had an accident, so I quit the fast stuff."

Fast stuff indeed. His hard work and talent netted him a brand new 1957 Corvette, 283 cubic inch, 4:11 positraction rear, 270 horsepower, three speed that I got to ride in as a kid who had never seen such a car. One night as we rode back into Bel Air on Rock Spring Road, Lowell downshifted from third to second without using the clutch. Then he took it down to first gear, still no clutch, just using the RPMs and tapping the accelerator. Never have before or since experienced such a maneuver. He was just a good driver, who knew everything the car was doing all the time.

Back to the '51. Currently a 232 cu. in. six cylinder, with a single barrel carburetor powers it. He drives it on weekends to the Spready Oak restaurant where he has breakfast. Originally it was a sort of metallic gray and maroon, and that's where he hopes to take her back.

Managing a life-long disease, Lowell looks back on growing up in Harford County pensively. "The thing I'm most proud of is that I could take something that someone didn't want 'cause it wouldn't run, and I could do something with it and turn it into something that did run, and looked good. Then it was something someone did want.

STH

Modest to a fault, soft spoken and thoughtful, the direct honesty and openness of this county homegrown is refreshing. On the farm, as a kid with a gift, it was him and his brother who had to fix machinery when it broke and there was a field to mow or corn to harvest. "I mean, if you were doing a job and something broke, you didn't call anybody, you had to figure out yourself what had to be done to finish the job."

"I lived by the adage, 'necessity is the mother of invention.' I can't remember all the things I did that turned out good, but they did."

========= 30 =========

Reminders – jot them here so you don't forget.

*   *   *

Tale of Two Tags

Something happened this morning that in a million years I would never have guessed...a phone call from a man I haven't seen in over a year...and at first I didn't recognize the voice. Actually thought it was my friend and still practicing veterinarian, Dr. Donald Merryman.

"Do you know who this is Todd?'

"Sure, how you doing Don?"

"Who? Did you just wake up?"

"No...you sound just like my veterinarian, Don Merryman."

"Well, this is John Probst, Whitey's brother, and I have something for you...from a long time ago. I'll be coming down with my brother Fred, and if you're gonna be home maybe we can stop by and give it to you."

"Sure, I'm here working outside. I'll be here, so just pull on up the lane. See you soon and drive safe!"

STH

When John showed up with Fred, he said there was
something that I had given his brother Whitey many,
many years ago. Of all things, it was a key tag that I had
made up and had given Whitey.

Looking into John's hands were two key tags and
they sure brought back a flood of memories. You see,
I actually dreamed them up when I first opened the
photography studio in Bel Air on Pennsylvania Avenue
back in 1972.

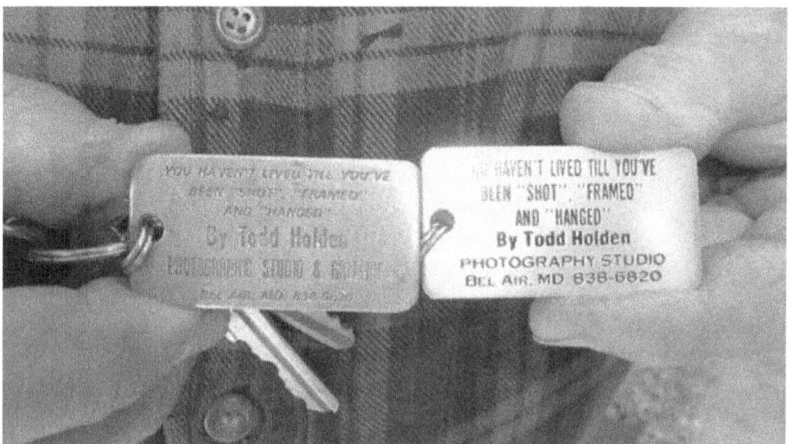

John Probst holds the two key tags that had been given to Whitey
and Punky Probst years earlier. Photo by Todd Holden.

I had wanted to get my name around that I was up
and at 'em in business and rather than have matches or
ballpoint pens or other stuff to hand out, I came up with
the aluminum key tag that would last and if cleverly
done, maybe, well, just maybe, folks would hang on to
them. Might even bring in a little business, which is
what those sort of things are for.

STH

Well, hang on to them they did...many friends still have the little tag, worn and faded, but still with the message that made folks laugh and keep our studio in mind.

My dad thought it was terrific and any time we can please our dads and get a big compliment, well that's hitting it out of the park.

On the tag it declared...

> *"YOU HAVEN'T LIVED TILL YOU'VE*
> *BEEN 'SHOT', 'FRAMED'*
> *AND 'HANGED'*
> *BY TODD HOLDEN*
> *PHOTOGRAPHY STUDIO*
> *BEL AIR, MD.   838-6820"*

It struck me that folks let me 'shoot' them, then they 'frame' and 'hang' the work in their homes or businesses. Might sound corny, but it caught on and I'd like to think it brought in a few customers.

The first batch cost me .20 cents each and I ordered 100 of them. Gave them to friends and then dad said, "Hell son, your friends already know you. Why not give them to folks you don't know and maybe they'll call for photography." Smart man, my dad.

Some of my friends still have the little key tags to this day and from time to time I hear from folks who remember them. Not exactly a collector's item, but

it was my pleasure to hand them out. So it was way
back then I gave two to Whitey and Punky Probst, who
lived on the farm next to Southampton. They had more
peafowl than any people I know...they were great pals
for many years.

   A couple years ago Punky passed away, and one year
ago this March, Whitey passed too. Brother John was
tending to Whitey on trips down from Pennsylvania, and
he took the little tag off of Whitey's key ring and put it
on his own.

   "Wanted a little reminder of brother, and this
   meant a lot to him, and now it does to me, Todd."

   Wow!! It blew me away that something given to
a friend so long ago had survived and actually been
cherished.

   When John was meeting with attorneys following
Whitey's death, one of them, Gregory Szoka, noticed
John had the little tag and said he knew me. John said
yes, he knew me too, that I was a good friend of his
brother for many years and had originally given it to
him.

   So the little tags survived. Whitey's was well worn,
but John found the 'fresh tag' that I had given to Punky,
and he gave it back to me the day he came down with
Fred.

STH

John and Fred Probst, a journey through time. Photo by Todd Holden.

Never thought in a million years that something like this would happen. It makes a body feel good when some little thing not of great value or significance is appreciated by someone else. Treasured...and then passed along to others.

Kind of makes you feel like we are really part of a much bigger thing going on in this world.

========= 30 =========

Here's your own blank slate for the day.

*   *   *

An Amazing Find

The tiniest frog I've ever seen, found in the driveway at Rustica.
Photo by Todd Holden.

A few years ago I wrote about an adult gray tree frog that was living in a white pine tree here at Rustica. I was lucky enough to spot the adult and take a photograph of it. Each night I could hear several calling.

Not often seen on the ground or at water's edge, except in breeding season, they may forage aloft, chiefly in small trees or shrubs, that are near or actually standing in shallow bodies of water. Such was not the case here beside the tool shed and fire pit, but there are rain barrels for watering plants and flowers.

Tree frogs are extremely well camouflaged while they are clinging to the bark of a rough tree trunk. Most times, like many creatures, their presence is known only when they call. The call of the tree frog is unmistakable,

STH

a musical trill, sometimes resembling the call of a red-bellied woodpecker actually. I had not seen, but only heard the tree frogs this season. There were several but none as close as the one I observed a couple years ago...

Then, one early evening while my editor was over and was about to leave did I spot this tiny 'pea' on the drive way. The sun had already set and the only light came from the garage, but something was there. It looked like a piece of the millings and yet it was different. I must congratulate Dr. Chuck Castora, who made my eyes like new with laser surgery.

I picked the tree frog up to inspect it; sure enough feet were just forming. I couldn't believe it was alive, so small and so calm. It's a lucky thing a bird or mouse didn't see this tiny creature before I did. Standing in the night light gazing upon something so tiny and beautiful. No pun intended, but...it's the little things.

Maybe not the biggest deal in the grand scope of nature, but seeing this little guy was a testimony to the stewardship maintained here at Rustica. So many things go unnoticed by so many, and just by looking up, or looking down, we can see what is in the world around us. Makes me proud to be the caretaker on this small parcel of earth, fostering an environment for all manner of wildlife to live peacefully and to thrive. I have always taken that task seriously and holding that little fella in the palm of my hand was a reward beyond expectations.

========== 30 ==========

STH

Don't Mess Around
With Kenny Cantler

Young Kenny Cantler with his prized Chevrolet. Not someone to be messed with.

A traveling and working pal of the late Allen 'Bud' Lloyd, Kenneth Cantler was there for it all and then some, when it came to his life and times.

Many years ago, a young and tough Louis 'Kenkaid' Scotten was rousing it up at the pool table one night with another patron at the Veterans of Foreign Wars hall on the east end of town.

STH

Kenny Cantler was tending bar that night and with his 'barkeep's perception' saw that real trouble could erupt at any time, thus affecting the meager tips he mustered on a shift.

"Next thing I know is Kenny comes over and reaches around with one arm and picks me up by the scruff of my neck, lifts me off the floor and walks me outside and deposits me on the parking lot," Scotten relates today from his home on Atom Road, Delta.

Kenkaid greatly admired Cantler in spite of that 'airlift' from the pool table. "He was one helluva man. The dining room walls here in this house were done by Kenny Cantler, years ago, and look at them today. Perfect!"

Then there was a fella by the name of Eb 'Ebhart' Flaherty at the bar one night when Kenny was tending. Eb was a 'finger pointer, a finger waver'...and he's doing his thing and Kenny brings up a 'ready-to-go mousetrap' and catches the finger in it, to the yell of Eb and the delight of everyone else at the bar.

The obvious take away to all of this is that Kenneth Cantler was someone you just didn't mess with. Back in the day when life was perhaps a simpler notion and living in a small town was the norm, Ken stood tall where and when it was needed. The adventures almost outweigh the man, but not quite. To anyone who knew him, he was one of the nicest guys around.

STH

This is part two of the saga of two of Delta's finest men...both now long gone, Allen "Bud" Lloyd and Kenneth Cantler. A number of readers have commented on the story of Bud Lloyd and since that piece was published, many have passed along stories of another great Deltonian, Kenneth Cantler. The two were a pair. They worked together, fought all comers together, drank together and were lifelong pals. Their legacy continues to grow, and I'm compelled to share Kenny's story.

As with any larger than life character, there will likely be a few blanks in the particulars and even more likely a few adventures not told. An appreciation of his life is the intent...and I'm sure hoping I get it right, because I don't want to mess with Kenny.

Kenneth Cantler was born on July 13, 1920, in Cardiff, Maryland and grew up in Skunk Hollow on Ridge Road in Whiteford, Maryland. His parents were Elwood and Beulah Cantler. Kenneth had two sisters, Mary Faile and Beverly LeMaster, and one brother, Donald. As a young man, like so many Americans, he proudly did his duty with the military.

He served overseas in WWII during the years 1942-1945. When he came of age, he was six feet tall and weighed 200 pounds. When he died at the age of 63, he was still six feet and weighed 200 pounds. Along the way, there were plenty of fights and, yes, I suppose that's the first thing that comes to mind when his name comes up.

STH

Yet, Kenny was a happy man, uncluttered by the
burdens that plague many young men. He knew who he
was and was comfortable in his skin. He worked hard,
lived hard, and enjoyed life with just as much grit.

Kenneth and Bradford Cantler at William Watters Church in
Coopstown in an undated photo.

In 1953, Kenny married Bradford Hinegardner and
they raised two daughters, Linda Cantler-Donhauser
and Donna Cantler. In later years, he also had one
granddaughter that he adored, Heather Fluck. At the
time of his death he was employed at Genstar, the
Churchville quarry. He had a heart attack while sitting
in a dump truck.

STH

His nephew, Alan LeMaster, recalls this tragic day. "I remember the dark day in October of 1983, Dad and I working on a garage in Delta. Donnie Tarbert, very visibly shaken, came running up to Dad, and telling him to get home and take care of Mom, that Uncle Kenny had died while working that afternoon. For me, the world seemed to tilt off center and I couldn't quite get it right in my head. Uncle Kenny always seemed in great shape and he never complained but as far as I know he also never went to a doctor so who knows.

"He loved baseball and softball, and played basketball at Slate Ridge School," continues Alan. "I understand that he played a lot of sports when he was young and that he was very good. He threw right handed and batted left. He could do tricks with a baseball, like releasing it from his hand, rolling it down the inside of his forearm, and snapping his bicep against the ball, popping it into the air and catching it with the other hand.

"He loved to hunt and fish. We fished together a lot when I was little. He never ran out of patience, even after I'd gotten my fishing line tangled for the 100th time. I'd call out for his help and he'd say "All-right, fish with my pole while I get you fixed up." Most times when he handed me his rod, he would have a fish already hooked and I'd bring it in while he untangled my mess. He always let on that I caught the fish all on my own. He was good about giving others the credit. He was happy just to see his family and friends being happy.

STH

"He was always smiling, laughing, cutting up and
one of the friendliest persons I've ever known. He liked
people and everyone that I know liked him."

According to seasoned writer and purveyor of
life, Mack Lloyd, son of Allen 'Bud' Lloyd, Kenny was
contented with life. "I don't ever remember seeing
Kenny when he wasn't laughing or smiling. He had a
great sense of humor and he liked to have fun," says
Mack.

"Kenny was working for Dad, prior to the time he
got married," continued Mack. "He was as strong as
they come. As a kid, I remember being on a plastering
job with Dad, working on a new home. The front porch
steps still hadn't been built, so planks were laid to reach
up to the framed-in doorway on a steep incline. Kenny
had mixed rough-coat plaster and filled four five-gallon
buckets to carry inside for Dad and the other guys to
trowel onto the walls and ceilings.

"Most men tote plaster with one heavy bucket in each
hand at a time, but Kenny wasn't like most men. He
doubled the load, walked up the steep planks, and lifted
those buckets up to almost shoulder height to angle
through the doorway, turning to wink at me. Whether
he was putting on a show to impress me or hefting those
buckets naturally, the man was strong as an ox."

Kenny sometimes helped his father, Elwood Cantler
tend bar at the "old" Whiteford Legion and later he
tended bar regularly at the Delta VFW in the 60s and 70s,

which included the time when the Peach Bottom nuclear plant was built and some rough construction boys came to town. Kenny was pretty good at keeping things under control when the boys got riled. He'd ask you nicely to hold down the cursing or carrying on, or if he had to "flag" you and ask you to leave, he'd tell you to come back tomorrow, no problem. However, if you refused to cooperate he could handle that also. He could put one hand on the bar and jump over it to the other side. Fast.

Mack Lloyd noted, "With Kenny, it wasn't just the fighting that he earned a reputation for, but folks knew him as a good man. There was the time late one night (or very early morning) after he had closed the VFW in Delta where he tended bar, Kenny was driving through Cardiff on his way home when he noticed flames inside the Terry Togs sewing factory, located on Main Street. He rushed into our house to alert the Delta-Cardiff VFD. It turned out to be a huge fire which destroyed the building. There were fire trucks from as far away as Stewartstown. Kenny's quick action most likely saved several nearby homes from being destroyed, as well.

"Kenny was also a great whistler," concludes Mack. "He could imitate songbirds better than anyone around."

Another Delta sage, Ron Roberts remembers Kenny. "My father and Kenny grew up together over in 'The Hollow', just east of town over the slate ridge. They were lifelong buddies. I used to visit him at the VFW where he worked and he would tell me 'back in the day' stories all night long.

STH

"There were some tough characters around town back in the 40s and 50s, but Kenny Cantler was arguably the toughest of them all. His pugilistic skills were something to behold, yet he was always a perfect gentleman, recalls Ron."

Kenny's daughter, Linda Cantler-Donhauser, who provided much of the family details, adored her father very much. "I have heard all the stories about his drinking and fighting but I didn't know that side of him because he quit drinking when he was 32 years old and never touched the stuff again.

"My fondest memories of him are when he wanted Donna and I to come in the house he didn't yell for us, he whistled. I use to love going fishing with him and especially going and setting lines for snapping turtles."

The great Jack Grafton, a revered Deltonian and friend of both Kenny and Bud Lloyd says, "He was the most feared fist fighter in the county...he was not to be messed with...he had the notoriety as the nicest guy in the world, unless you challenged him or crossed him.

"As I recall, he'd go to Little Falls on Route 1 and some guys who had a little too much would want to challenge him...Kenny would swing once or twice and the guy was done.

"His brother, Duck Cantler, was killed in an accident at the Emory Church intersection. It's hard to lose a brother no matter how it happens. Sometime later,

STH

Ken Cantler with daughter Linda Cantler-Donhauser. The two
enjoyed fishing together as shown here in an early photo.

there was a guy at Little Falls who made a comment
disrespecting Duck. Kenny waited for him later to take
him out, but the guy never showed.

"Ken Cantler was personable; likable...they just don't
make 'em like him anymore."

STH

Nope, Ken Cantler was someone you just did not
want to mess with. If there had been fisticuffs between
Ken and Bud Lloyd, it is likely the two would still be
swinging and there'd be no reason to lay a bet. Yet,
the two were a pair and it's unlikely they ever would
have fought...and beyond all this talk of fighting, these
gentlemen stood tall on many other merits. No, they
don't grow 'em like that anymore...but it's sure a good
thing we had Mr. Cantler around to keep things straight.

I never really knew either one of them, although I
have heard Bud's voice when he would make a telephone
call late at night, and my grandmother Addie Holden
would be working the switchboard at the telephone
exchange. I can still hear his voice, "Now Aunt Addie,
I've got to help this guy out...please connect me."

We need heroes while we grow up and I had plenty to
choose from and learn from...many of Delta's men would
be heroes to me if only I had gotten the chance to know
them better. Through this writing I have been able to
do just that. Perhaps after reading this, the same will be
true for you.

========= 30 =========

Thanks to Ken's nephew, Alan LeMaster for anecdotal references,
Linda Cantler- Donhauser, Kenny's oldest daughter, for priceless
insight and familial connections and to Bev and Bill LeMaster,
Kenny's sister and brother-in-law for photo submissions. – Todd
Holden

A Ride To Reuben's

REUBEN'S DRIVE IN Route U.S. 1. BEL-AIR, Md.

No other place like it...before or since. A post card of Reuben's Drive In when the gas pumps thrived. Photographer unknown.

Mike Coale was a good buddy of mine, from the days at St. Margaret School, where he was a grade ahead of me and from the biggest, toughest family on the street where I lived.

First day I ever saw the Coale's they were playing baseball in the middle of Broadway Extended, and I came riding through on my bike while my folks were unloading the moving van.

Riding around the block, I came upon that same game with the Coale's...I kept pedaling and a ball was hit, came right by me, and someone yelled, "Hey you, get the ball!"

STH

I did not, mainly because they looked scary. They were mostly bigger than me and it was my first hour on what would also become my home turf for seven years.

They embraced me that day, sort of a baptism by fire, and one of them, maybe Dukey, threw a rock at me. It hit me squarely in the back and sent me home crying.

My dad didn't do a thing, cause to tell the truth I think even he was afraid of the Coale's.

Years passed. We moved to the farm and so did the Coale's, to their farm south of Darlington. Mike went on to become one of the best football players to ever grace the field at Bel Air High School and then Coach Cesky saw to it that Mike Coale got a full scholarship to University of Maryland.

Mike was so good as a university freshman, the varsity toughs ganged up on him, made his life a living hell, and Mike as a gentle guy in a giant's body, said to hell with it, and he came back home to Harford County.

He got a job at Bata Shoe Company, and with some folks he was known as the Bata Bear....a name he did not cotton to. I never called him that. After all, I missed a softball, and got hit in the back, why even utter a slang his way, especially if I was riding in his car, getting a lift somewhere.

STH

And so it came to be I was attending University of Maryland and was home for a weekend with no car. Mike came by Southampton and picked me up to cruise Reuben's and the flats up near Mount Tabor Church on Route 1, where lots of great drag races were held.

Mike and I pull into Reuben's and across the way from us is Jimmy Thornton, in his Chevy ragtop. Jimmy was kind of a jerk, but he had the prettiest lady with him and Mike and I wanted to find out who she was.

Mike pulls alongside of Jimmy and says hi and we both are checking out the brunette in the red sweater and plaid skirt...she was a knockout. Jimmy did not introduce us to his lady friend, but she was on both Mike's and my mind.

I'd never seen eyes like hers before...she absolutely knocked me out. Mike was not as forward as me, and when I asked Jimmy who his new friend was, he laughed, rolled up the window and turned away.

So Mike cranks up his car and backs up and around to the other side, the side where she was sitting...and the side I was sitting on.

I looked at this beauty, Mike smiled a sheepish grin, as if to say, "O.K. big shot, make your move, cause I'm getting hungry for a steakburger!" I looked at her, her window down, and said my name, and asked her for hers. "Ann," she said, "Ann Newman." She turned away, Jimmy fired the Chevy up and they drove away.

STH

I was smitten. Next day, a Saturday, I called every Newman in the phone book, everyone, from Al Newman all the way to Monroe Horace Newman, 419 Roberts Way, Aberdeen. I called them all, and whoever answered the phone, I asked for Ann. Needless to say, there were lots of hang-ups and "Nobody here by that name."

Until a woman answered and when I asked for Ann... she said, "Just a minute" and as she turned from the phone, I could hear her say, "Ann, darling, it's for you."

I asked her for a date and she said she was booked all weekend and the next weekend. So I asked about the next weekend and she said "Okay." And where did we go? Of course to Reuben's in my dad's Mercury Station Wagon and Mike was there and he saw me with my prize. He laughed and gave me a nod of approval for a mission accomplished. Not too many years later, Ann and I married.

And to the day when I last saw Mike, in his van at Boe's 7-11 in Bel Air, we recalled that episode and laughed, and when I heard he finally gave in to a series of battles that would have killed a lesser man a lot sooner, I was deeply saddened.

He was part of my life, even though our social paths did not cross, he was still my friend. I will never forget him or that autumn night at Reuben's Drive In.

========== 30 ==========

STH

Sam, III and Me

S am said he was 'gonna roll the dice' as we
finished up a plate of raw oysters at the Slate
Ridge American Legion. On his mind was Hank
Williams III, grandson of the legendary Hank Williams,
who was appearing a few hours later at the Chameleon
Club in downtown Lancaster. Sam had spent some time
with him two nights before in Baltimore and was bound
and determined to photograph him.

We had no tickets, just a seize-the-moment kind of
thing. Sam had his camera and gear to take some shots
and we were set to spin the wheel. I've heard III's music,
liked it, well, most of it, and said 'count me in.' After a
quick call to my buddy to get him to tend to the pups, we
were set for the ride north.

In another lifetime, it was me barreling down
the road to take pictures of some show. Sam would
sometimes accompany me and sure enough, he, too,
soaked in the pure joy of capturing an image of an icon
on the fly. The honor has been all mine to stand in the
company of some of the greats. But more on that later.

We hit the town in no time flat. I hadn't been up
Lancaster way in a year or more, when I rode with
Mackie Lloyd and Sam to see the great George "No
Show" Jones at the American Music Theater. Well,
there's a big difference between the two venues as well
as the performers.

STH

George is rounding the bend on a great career. His voice is almost what it used to be and it was a great show, just to see the man in person, which I also did with my family when I was very young at the New River Ranch, near Colora.

Hank III is country, with a punk-ass attitude and a voice as distinct as any singer around. He's got a sound to him that recalls Hank Sr., but by all accounts, he's his own man.

A short while after Sam made contact with the tour manager while I tended to the car and equipment, we were escorted backstage where the band was. Simple as that we were transported back maybe three decades.

I helped Sam with his setup lighting and distances. That done, Sam was primed for the 'deal' and it all brought back to me the days of shooting Waylon Jennings, Willie Nelson, Johnny Paycheck, Sonny James, oh man, I can't remember the rest just now...lots of good musicians though.

The Holden travel case. The smell of cordovan leather still brings back the memories. Photo by Todd Holden.

STH

Backstage passes are like
manna from heaven for the
musician photographer.
Photo by Todd Holden.

For the night, we did what
so many dads and sons never
get to do...reverse roles. All
those years ago, Sam sat and
watched as I set things up
and you might say, learned
the craft. I'm a bit slower
these days, of course, but still
going strong...and to be in the
company of my son as he does
his own take on things, well,
the feeling is priceless.

We only had a little over 5
minutes to shoot Hank before
he took the stage at 9 sharp.
He's on time, and before his
arrival the other band members rolled into the cramped
backstage area where we were to do the shoot.

The band is cool, very easy to meet and greet,
chatting about haircuts, overcoming the anticipation
of hitting the stage shortly in front of a beer-drinking,
rowdy crowd.

In walks Hank looking like an escapee from Dachau,
in shredded black jeans, held together with bedding-
safety pins, pale as porcelain, straighter than a laser...he
came to play and not just for the ride...stretched over that
six-foot frame is a lot of country and bad-ass.

STH

Sam introduces me to Hank, we shake hands. As he talks, Hank III is as appreciative, cordial and courteous as any man from the South can be...he impressed me in that brief encounter. He is definitely the leader of the band and the spawn of greatness, passed down from generations of soul piercing, hard picking and heart throbbing music that is as American as it gets.

We do our shoot quickly and it's show time as the band single files up the narrow steps to the stage amid thunderous applause.

Last in line flowing out onto the stage Hank III says flatly..."If you don't like gettin' pushed around up close to the stage, you ought not to get this close.'

He then mentioned the fans, giving credit to the working class folks who like his music and pointing out that money is hard to come by for most of us, and that's the reason for the $16 and $18 tickets to his show tonight.

With that, he jumped right into a hard-driving country number and it took off from there. Myself, I lean to the country side of Hank 3, as he now likes to be known, but I've heard some of the punk stuff and well, it does have an attitude. For obvious reasons, when he was first starting out making records, his record label wanted to market him as Nashville's latest incarnation of his grandfather. But Hank 3 was having none of that.

STH

Hank III, the country punk who knows where he comes from, on stage at the Chameleon Club, Lancaster, PA. Photo by Sam Holden.

Sure, he knows and can certainly play a country song as good as anybody from down South that sings and plays a guitar. But he also has played drums in punk rock bands and even plays a little thing called punk-a-billy.

He generally mixes his shows up with the different genres and never looks back. Hank 3 and his band roll from one song to the next with fury. They say seeing him and his band live is like cowboys with Mohawks or punks sporting Stetsons. No matter, he plays like he means it and rolls out each number like it's his last.

Like he states on his website, "I've always taken the hard road. That's what makes us different and what gives the wide audience range of 14 to 80. Cowboys, punks, metalheads, jocks, grandmas, and the average everyday person – we bring them all together under the same roof. That's what makes us proud. That's what makes it worth it at the end of the day." Any generation of Hank could smile at that.

STH

Everything dies, baby, that's a fact
But maybe everything that dies
S o m e d a y ,   c o m e s   b a c k

Atlantic City, by Bruce Springsteen
and performed by Hank Williams III

   History was made and that's a fact. Not so much in
the sense of getting pictures of Hank Williams III, which
is pretty good in and of itself. Not really that I got in to
see a show where rolling the dice was the deuce in the
hole, although the memories are significant. The night
was special simply because we were all in a moment of
greatness...Sam, III and me.

========= 30 =========

The next time Sam shot III, first thing he asked was, "How's your
dad?" Warms my heart to this day.

Stockpiling Some Peace of Mind

Throughout the summer storms, hurricanes, big winds and trees that just couldn't 'stand anymore,' no pun intended, my son and his pal, Ralph, have amassed a supply of firewood for heat this winter.

Sam heats with wood in our studio in Little Italy in Baltimore. One of the prime stoves came from Will Pardew. It's an old Army surplus 'barrack pot-bellied stove'...and can use coal or wood. It really throws the heat out. These stoves did their job keeping the boys warm in those drafty WWII barracks and they still earn their stripes.

All told there are three stoves in the studio keeping the place a pleasant, draft-free, 71 degrees on the coldest day we've had so far this winter. Sam says, "bring it."

The stockpile of firewood doesn't come by happen-stance however. Throughout the summer, on some pretty hot days, and on into the fall, the

Will Pardew and the pot-bellied stove.
Photo by Todd Holden.

STH

trees that have been blown down are cut up, split and stored here at Rustica. Whenever someone calls with a tree that's down and needs to be removed, Sam and crew jump at it.

We don't have a truck to haul the wood, we have friends who do, so everyone wins...trees accumulated this year were ash, white and pin oak, locust, cherry and sycamore. We also have cut up tulip poplar and that's what we give our friends who have chimera stoves on their patios, where the fire is mainly for looks, not heat. Seems every year, more tulip poplars blow over here in our woods, and we clear it, cut it, and store it till someone needs some wood for a fire pit or special occasion.

The fire pits here at Rustica are primitive and functional, serving as gathering places for those who visit and enjoy stoking the logs. Good therapy so I'm told.

Taking the chill off. Lady Frisco, Lord Nelson and Prince Chesterfield enjoy the #2 fire pit on the lane to the pond. Photo by Sam Holden.

STH

My daughter's family has a huge iron 'fire pit' on
their patio, a favorite gathering spot to huddle around
before and after dinners there. All ages share a spot
around the fire...sometimes no one utters a sound, we
are all transfixed by the fire and the warmth it provides.

A friend of mine is building a fire pit at his home in
Homestead Village. Seems every time he comes to visit
of late we start a fire with some old papers from the
trash. The fire pit just seems to draw good souls like a
moth is drawn to a flame.

Some nights it's just too cold to sit out by the fire;
nonetheless, we start one, share a moment or two, maybe
a story, before someone gives up to head home or inside.

Just before the chill of late fall took hold, a massive
Saturday job of stacking and splitting occurred that went
a little beyond our expectations. We were happy about
the wood and had fun getting it stacked.

The load shown on the next page included cherry
and locust. Thank God we found a wood splitter at
Paul Burkheimer's a couple years ago, because using a
mall and wedges would be rough with logs this size.
The splitter is a back-saving tool. Usually you can find
a good one for under $1000 and they are well worth it,
saving wear and tear on the back.

STH

A little wood goes a long way. Photo by Todd Holden.

A little philosophy in doing the wood for yourself.
Bob Callahan told me years ago, "He who heats with
wood is warmed by it many times...when he cuts it, then
splits it, then stacks it, then burns it."

True, but it will take some work and planning. Then
you have the peace of mind of knowing you'll have
enough heat for whatever the winter months bring.

========= 30 =========

STH

Getting Ready For Surgery

After years of dealing with bad knees from previous injuries and old age, the time has come to handle the problem, with major surgery. All the years of kneeling on the left knee while shooting the Baltimore Colts in Memorial Stadium took a toll for sure...but in those days you had to be on one knee or you might catch a beer bottle in the head from fans on the sideline seats.

I always played by the rules, never got smacked and got some great photographs during my tenure with the team.

Playing golf one day with my late pal, Billy Marshall, I blew out the left knee on a follow through and it took me down to the ground. That began a series of cortisone injections and finally laparoscopic surgery to buy me a little more time. I was told by the surgeon that it might help for a couple years, no guarantees.

Friends have urged me to just get the knees replaced, 'no big deal' and all that stuff. The last couple of years, just as the cortisone relief would wear off and I had to deal with the pain big time, I convinced myself to follow through with the surgery.

Then, a few weeks would go by, maybe another shot of cortisone, and I was good to go. The knees would be better, but only in spurts. Still couldn't play golf, or tennis, or walk a lot on rough ground.

"Is this the way you want to live out your life Dad, with limping, pain, no sports? It's only gonna get worse," cautioned my son Sam. My daughter Mina was less forceful, since her husband has had several knee operations and is still holding off on 'full knee replacement.'

Thinking it was time, and truly the knees were getting much worse, I checked with a couple friends who recommended getting it done. One was Robbie Martin, who has been on my case for more than a year. Ultimately, I went to his orthopedic surgeon, Dr. Brian Mulliken, for a second opinion.

I made the decision that day to get it done.

Figuring this time of year would give me a chance to take it easy with chores indoors here at Rustica, with a little therapy I'd be ready to roll come spring and the tasks that time of year brings.

One major problem still needed addressing...my pups. For those who know me and who've read my columns, you know my pups are my immediate family. I've noted before that I regard myself more as a caretaker here at Rustica for the wildlife and for the pups.

No matter, with the knee surgery already scheduled, my four-legged family had to be taken care of while I was in the hospital, maybe up to a week. Mina said she'd take care of Lady Frisco, and Sam said he'd keep Little Dude and Chester. Sounded good, but as I've come closer to the date of surgery I have begun to worry about the pups and their adjusting to new surroundings if only for a short time.

This morning I wrote a note to Mina...just thinking of the little things to help Frisco with her visit to Mina's.

"While it's on my mind Mina...a couple things that will make the time spent w/Lady Frisco better in a temporary home.

"She always goes into your woods, behind the utility shed to pooh...she never poohs in the yard here...just the way I trained her...so...in the a/m or last call at night, just walk her out to the woods, say 'pee pee'...and she will be fine.

"Only time she growls is feeding time, and that's usual for an older pup...she nibbles, rarely eats all her food at one time...in the a/m I give her her pill for joints, soak it in water, so it's more palatable for her.

"She sleeps on my bed every night and I know that might not suit you, so if she's put somewhere warm, just an old blanket will be fine.

"As she's gotten older she drinks more water...goes with the age...I'm sure you know all of this, but I'm concerned about her while I'll be out of the loop...and just a few helpful tips will make everyone happy.

"I'm worried about surgery big time...and scared too.

"I'll think of some other stuff, just me being me.

"I just worry about the pups...and if you know their little patterns, like humans, all will be better.

Love you,"
Dad

So it goes, I'll craft another note to Sam to help him with Little Dude and Chester as the fears arise of not being with my pups...that's the real bitch for me...we've grown so used to each other's behaviors and company. While I'm recovering in the hospital before I come home, it'd be great if they were there right after the surgery.

Maybe I can talk one of my pals into a little adventure.

========= 30 =========

Editor's Note: As of this writing, Birdman has gone through surgery with flying colors. He won't be dancing the fandango anytime soon, but he has been reunited with his pals, Frisco, Dude, and Chester. And for certain, he wouldn't have made it through without his other real family, Sam and Mina.

Target Bird For The Day

F or many years, whether driving cars or tractors, back roads or fields, I almost always would spot several American kestrels either perched on telephone wires or hovering over a soon to be meal along the roads and fields.

Lately though, I haven't really seen any. So I got to wondering, with the abundance of red-tail and red-shoulder hawks, plenty of Cooper's and sharp-shinned hawks...why not so many kestrel's anymore.

Some folks claim they see them all the time. I'm not sure why it is when I travel to Delta, most every Sunday, I don't see a kestrel on the back roads traveling home. I could always count on seeing at least one on the ride.

I asked Les Eastman who's kind of a wheel with the Harford County Bird Club what he thought.

"It's probably habitat reduction. They prefer open grassy or shrubby areas. With the decline of farming and the rise of developments, they don't have as many places to hunt.

"Also, they are cavity nesters. People are less inclined to leave dead or damaged trees alone these days to allow cavities to be created. Putting out more

STH

nest boxes might help," Les wrote. He also added two locations where a sighting was pretty much guaranteed. Trappe Church Road just a bit past Deth's Ford Road was on the money. Sure enough, as I cruised recently, there was a female kestrel, plump, sitting on wires, flitting on down the line, then across an open meadow to another set of wires leading to a farm house.

This is the amazing thing about birding and birders; usually if a bird is content in its habitat they will remain pretty punctual on the rounds. This was true for the rare red-headed woodpecker that used to hang on Davis road at Geneva Farm Golf Course. For years it was there, then one spring it was no more.

Les added another location for the kestrel...

"I saw 2 kestrels today," he mentioned. "The first one was about 2 PM along Rock Run Road. It was hovering over the pasture across the road from the small pond. Location is on the right as you go towards Susquehanna State Park.

"The second one I saw about 3:30 on Trappe Church Road west of Darlington. It was sitting on the wire about a quarter mile west of the intersection of Deth's Ford Road. It has been there for several months so it must be finding plenty of food. I hope it got counted on the Christmas Count."

STH

'The little hawk on the telephone wire.' Photographer unknown.

There you have it...if you've never seen a kestrel, you know where to go for a nice drive in the country. The kestrel is the smallest falcon in North America...actually not a 'hawk' per se. Still we refer to them as 'the little hawk on the telephone wires'...seems to fit because that's where we usually see them, when we see them.

STH

They are an interesting bird to watch and I'm glad Les came through with some good advice. Let's hope all their habitat isn't lost.

========= 30 =========

All A Mistake

As I slowly recover from double-knee surgery, I am recuperating at my son Sam's place where everyone can keep an eye on me. Believe me, it's well appreciated. I'm getting stronger all the time and can't wait to get home to my own creature comforts. There was a time I dreaded this surgery, believing it was going to be one big mistake. Then again, mistakes happen for a reason.

The other day I was relaxing after a morning of physical therapy and had finished reading the book I had. The free time got me to thinking on how certain things came about just by making a mistake.

Some of the best things we do creatively come about because of a miscalculation or a forgotten ingredient. These mistakes don't always pan out. When we bake sometimes the outcome can be pretty bad. The horrible taste likely happened because we left out something critical.

Even more of a slip-up, God forbid the surgeon leaves something out when they are sewing you back up or accidentally leaves the scissors in. You get the idea.

But every now and then we are just winging things and the outcome is better than we had planned, and it was due to a 'mistake'...mostly unintentional.

STH

In high school art class, Mr. Anthony Hyde was my teacher, and my project was to do an oil painting of either a seascape or a landscape...I chose a landscape.

It was in my mind, of windmills, water and cloudy skies. I was 13 and had never had an art class so this was a moment of clarity. We painted on masonite boards, choosing the rough-surfaced side. Mixing the oils after priming the piece of masonite I sketched in the windmills, and where the water and sky would go.

Mixing the oils offered me some colors I never imagined, taking me a little off course in the reality department. Who was I to know the color of windmills? I knew the colors of the sky, clouds and water....so the painting was done.

I gave the finished landscape to Miss Alice Bennington, a co-worker at the telephone company and friend of my grandmother, Addie Holden. Alice cherished that painting, hanging it in her hallway. She and Henry told Addie how much they appreciated the windmills and sky...offered up by a first-time painter.

The mistakes in the 'realism' of the painting are long forgotten. When Alice passed away, the little painting was offered back to me, and now it hangs on the wall in my home. A little reminder of what I created at an early age...a lot of sentimental value in that little painting.

Later on in life I wanted to learn photography and started out with a co-worker at the *Aegis*, Bill Whitman.

STH

We both helped each other set up a little darkroom in the men's room at the newspaper. We had to wait until after 5 p.m. when most of the office staff went home.

With just the editorial staff, which consisted of me, Bill, Tom Penrod and Robbie Wallis, there wasn't a lot of action in the men's room, and we had running water, hot and cold, and developing tanks for film. Next was setting up an enlarger, one that I found at the Camera Mart on Harford Road in Hamilton. That was it for the men's room darkroom, and Bill and I later set up another darkroom in the basement of my home.

Sometimes we made mistakes in developing times and printing chemistry, but the outcome wasn't always bad, matter of fact, sometimes it was extraordinary. Textures came about from not agitating the film in the developer. These images, later on when they were printed, gave us a lift from the ordinary.

When something really worked well, we noted what we did, as we did with all processing and printing, while we were learning. Later on, when I turned professional, there was still time spent experimenting on the fun stuff and creative subjects I chose.

My son Sam was usually in the darkroom at some point when I was printing, and he caught on to the process of making images on paper, through the use of light, camera and chemistry. Today, he has carried the ball forward from those days of me and him printing in the darkroom and like me he has taken 'experimental

STH

side trips' to see what color does when the film is over-
or under-developed, or printed on different kinds of
paper.

He has exhibited his creative work coast to coast, and
stays busy for the next adventure. The image shown
on the opposite page is a cross-processed example.
The ingredients are a closely guarded secret, and the
chemicals and paper are becoming harder and harder to
find, due to the advent of digital photography.

Most of the commercial work he does is digital and
that keeps the bill collector's away from the door. It's
the fun stuff that he and I did over the years that affords
release from a 'job' in that we make the rules for the
subject and the outcome.

Sam and I have both been asked to do commercial
work for clients, and near the end of the shoot, we ask if
we can try a couple other techniques, once the 'money
shot' is in the can. Most times the clients are more than
willing to let us try some things on our own.

Sometimes, the clients end up preferring what we
'experimented' with from what they had originally asked
for. That's a good thing, because they end up with a
'straight image' for all manner of usage, and another
image that offers a little look into a spectrum of colors
and shapes that seem to never age or be out of place.

A fine example of cross-processing photography is shown here with one of Delta's own, Kenny Scotten. Photo by Sam Holden.

The little mistakes sometimes become 'big intentional techniques'...that's a fact. With free time and some quality recollection over, I think I'll get out of this chair and take a stroll.

========= 30 =========

These pages are beautiful mistakes...can you think
of any you've made and they turned out fine?

*   *   *

Affairs In Order

If you've read my columns regularly, you pretty much know that I write what I feel, what's on my mind, and what's going on now. I'll take on historical projects in the manner of character studies of some of our local icons like Ken Cantler.

Of course, I have always been comfortable looking back to the simpler times that so many of you recall, but also in the hopes that some of that old common sense will rub off on some of the younger readers.

Here of late though, I've basically been a shut-in, at least by my standards. The Sunday drives are coming back, but there's a lot to be done here at Rustica that I just can't risk doing right now. For the most part, I've been patient.

By now you may be sick and tired of reading of my adventures with double knee-replacement surgery in February. I've tried to write about all the other things this wonderful time of year brings and eventually I'll be back in the swing. Really though, this latest journey has been so all consuming, well, it just needs mentioning.

If all this talk of knees has begun to bore you, well, there's always the obits and classifieds to make the Star worthwhile.

STH

Early on, I had been to two different orthopedic
surgeons. One had administered cortisone and draining
of the left knee. He also performed arthroscopic surgery
on the knee 5 years ago with the codicil that it might get
me relief for 'three or four years'...and that was just about
on the mark.

He was an okay surgeon, but I never really felt
comfortable after all he had done. Besides, there were
days, honest and true, when the left knee was fine. I
could clean, walk, do chores without any pain at all.
"Maybe surgery really isn't necessary," I began to tell
myself. After a few days of wonderful relief, like after
a cortisone shot, when there was no pain and total
freedom of movement, I felt invincible. Those days made
life worth living, and revitalized me.

All good things change and over and over, after a few
months of comfort, the knee would act up and the pain
would return. Each time, the bout of pain lasted longer
and was more intense.

Eventually a friend recommended I see another
orthopedic surgeon for a second opinion, which I did...
and it was pretty much the same thing, concluding with
either a draining or a shot and then the words, "You will
know when to have the surgery, your knee will tell you."

That was all true. Still things were bad, and lots
of pain, just ask the pals I hang with. My buds from
the Delta Crew were totally frustrated with me for not
getting fixed up proper.

STH

And so it came to pass, on Christmas Eve at my daughter's, she and son Sam sat me down and helped to bring me out of 'surgical denial'. 'Do you want to live out the rest of your life not playing golf, not playing tennis, not walking the fields groundhog hunting?'

'Dad...it's only going to get worse. Next thing you'll be using a walker, or a cane, or worst of all, you'll wind up in a wheelchair.' Scary, huh? It was Christmas Eve and it felt like Halloween. But, we all hugged and they sent me home that night with books, some neat candles, nice clothing and words of wisdom.

Once I got home with Chester, Dude and Frisco there was some mighty soul searching. Still I wasn't sold on either of the two doctors I had seen.

Then, as if by karma, Robbie Martin ran into me up at Caneman's and again gave me the dickens for not getting the knee repaired. I had to tell him we were no longer talking of just the left knee as both were giving trouble.

Robbie told me he had both knees done by Dr. Brian Mulliken and was doing fine. Something to consider. About a week later I was buying some 'gift cards' at Enotria and the owner, Carlo Fortunato noticed me limping. He plays and coaches a lot of soccer in the county and said he had his knee done by Dr. Mulliken. Hmm...Next was Dr. Jose Gracia's wife, who had both knees and a hip done, by, you guessed it.

STH

The next day I called Dr. Mulliken's office and set up an appointment. The meeting went well and he echoed what the other surgeons had said, only he was more convinced the time had come for surgery. He was straight up and recommended full knee replacement...of both knees.

I called Mina and Sam with the news then got to thinking about horror stories from the past. About anesthesia, and folks getting daffy after surgery....

The choice was mine whether to do both at once and I waffled a bit, but eventually decided to go for it.

He set up surgery at St. Joe's for February 5th and February 8th.

Robbie Martin of course said it was no problem... Robbie of course is younger than me...and was enthusiastic that I had made the move. He also drummed into my head..."The operation is only 15% of the cure, the rehab and physical therapy is 85% of it...and you will be in pain, but have to do it religiously."

Of course, I didn't consider my rehab or what I was in store for, living in a two-story home, alone and with three pups. I had more pressing worries just getting the surgery...had no plan for what would happen afterward.

It was less than a month from surgery and my son decided he wanted to remodel the downstairs and provide me with a full bath, shower, bench seat...the works. He was not pleased that I hadn't considered all the post-surgery living arrangements when I booked the operation, but I told him it was leading with the heart and not the head, something I do often.

Sam and his assistants, Jeff and Bob Ewers went into action. I had to get my 'affairs in order,' sign and make copies of the living will...and a few more sobering documents.

We were moving along...

Next week's installments will carry on this long, slow, walk.

========= 30 =========

Here's another page for you.
*   *   *

Long, Slow Walk

Photo by Sam Holden.

Even on a bad day, you'll generally come into contact with folks from all walks of life. You may not engage the grocery clerk with so much as small talk and the postmaster may only get a nod and a thank you as the mail is handed over. You'll have days like this. Even then, you're still connected, you're still part of your world...the people, places, and things that surround you daily.

STH

Not so when you enter into the unknown world of doctors, nurses, strange feelings never felt before. Yes, it's an odd place to be in this feeling of not knowing what will come next, but knowing there's a risk of not returning...and that's even before the surgery.

I finally went through with my knee replacements. That's right, both at once. I wouldn't recommend getting both done for everyone, but I'm determined to be pain free and rather mobile by late spring. I went through surgery with flying colors they tell me. Immediate recovery slowly brought my focus around and I realized a couple of things.

First, I had indeed made it back to the world of the living. For anyone wishing otherwise, there won't be any wakes for me just yet. More importantly though, I realized just how alone I was. Just me and what's made it through 74 years of living and these two stiff and swollen knees.

Oh, I had folks around for sure. The doctors and nurses were good to me and my daughter and son have raised the bar big time for the love and care they've given me. Truth be told, besides my pups, I had all the company I needed. What Mina and Sam have done to help me, accommodate my idiosyncrasies, and be there for love and support means more to me than I can put into words.

STH

Beyond that, in the middle of the night or just about any time the mind is awake and begins to wander, I have felt so very detached from this earthly realm, separated from the daily rituals we all fall into. Never have been afraid to die, we all get there, but it's this otherworldly place I've been in that has changed a lot how I look at things.

The knees are on the mend. I'm putting one foot in front of the other and making it work. I've had setbacks and some bad days, but I'm now taking a long, slow walk back to the real world...back to the post office, the pals to see, the pups to take care of. Everything and then some.

========= 30 =========

J.D. Shellnut.

From what movie?

* * *

Don't Leave the Sunflower Bag In the Truck

When you see someone make a mistake, it's second nature to share your wisdom, perhaps make them all the wiser. When you make your own mistakes, it's also second nature to sort of keep it under wraps, don't want to speak ill of yourself.

Truth be known, I made a mistake and I'm not too proud to admit it. Hard to write this stuff, but it's all true and still unbelievable to a degree. A new one on me for sure. A bit of chronology is in order, so let me explain myself.

Back in December I stocked up on my one and only food for the bird feeders, black oil-based sunflower seed in the 50# bag from The Mill. Normally, I get dog food at the same time, but this time I didn't.

Lots going on at the time, making plans for the double knee replacements, lining up folks to tend the pups and keep an eye on the house...preparations took priority. As such, after my trip to The Mill, I forgot all about the bag of sunflower and it stayed in the back of the truck.

Fast forward to mid-March and I'm back home to recuperate...can't drive yet, but hobbling around the garage I notice the bag of sunflower still sitting in back

STH

of the truck. Have to mention also that I'm a fan of opening all the doors on the truck on nice days, nature's way of airing things out. Might have to re-think that.

As I look at the big sack in the back, I also see a tiny hole in the bag and lots of seed around. Carefully lifting the bag I thought nothing of the dire consequences soon to visit me.

Most times, but not this time, I keep the sunflower in a metal can in the tool shed. I went to tidy up and took the little vacuum out to clean up the mess in the truck. Then I noticed two things...the smell and the seed trail.

No one had been in the truck since February 1.

After being away so long and still on the mend, I wasn't allowed to drive, but knees or not it was time to put the sunflower bag in the tool shed metal container... albeit with a small hole in the side.

Gets better, or worse, depending on your perspective, but my troubles were only beginning. Those familiar little black specs, droppings from mice, were easily recognizable. The smell of rodent urine was also prevalent, but where was it coming from...under the seat, up in the ventilation system?

Rounding up the 'live traps' on hand and spreading napkins to detect the little visitors and lots of vacuuming kept me busy.

STH

Proper method to store black-oil-base sunflower seed, still in original bag, inside a metal garbage can. Dumping it out of bag into can, encourages bugs. Photo by Todd Holden.

After the first night, one large, female mouse was caught. Second night, a large male in the live trap. I was ecstatic, knowing that I had conquered the invasion.

By the way, those Victor old timey traps aren't worth the $1.97 for four of them. The mice ate the peanut butter, sprung the trap, and had a belly laugh on me. Tell you, those traps are worthless!!

Then things became a stale-mate...no more mice caught, no more trail of doo-doo across the napkins, but the smell was still there. Seemed like if both the mother and father had been caught, the children would scatter.

STH

Such was not the case. Apparently, the mice were smart enough to stockpile the sunflower seed somewhere in the truck. What was worse than knowing I still had mice was driving down the road with that rancid smell.

I concentrated on air fresheners and opening windows. The smell of vanilla wafted through the vehicle and I was hoping I could beat this thing.

Then I took off the extension on the vacuum and probed around under the seat to try to dislodge a nest, if there was one.

The days of opening up the car in the morning and the stench of rodent urine hitting me in the face have ceased actually...still, I'm not convinced the rodent hotel in my vehicle is now 'vacant.'

Idealistically, there is no nest...realistically, there's got to be one. So far, so good...perhaps I won't have to tear the upholstery out. There, it wasn't so bad to admit to a boo boo. Could've happened to anyone and now we're all the wiser.

========= 30 =========

Tempting the Lonely Heart

S ometimes fate, the cosmos, the tarot cards and a couple rolls of the dice bring about a conglomeration of emotions that would set a Hollywood scriptwriter on their ass. Love is that most unpredictable of emotions that almost certainly originated the act of 'throwing caution to the wind.' It is blind, or at the least, short-sighted. And speaking of wind, you can't see it when it hits you, but indeed you feel it.

Home is where my heart is...all of it. Photo by Ann Holden.

A pleasant wind will warm the heart, but an ill wind will cause pain, often too painful to endure.

Love certainly has a way of creating situations no one could dream of until they happen; no one could make them happen unless love's dream befalls you. You just can't make this stuff up, you become a player, a willing participant in this thing called love. It blows you like the wind and you make an attempt to embrace it.

STH

Only, like the wind, love is something quite difficult to harness and only a concerted effort by two willing participants could ever get their arms around such a force.

When only one person is working to harness the wind, so to speak, it is just too difficult a task. Perhaps the other person is only playing a game with the wind, dancing and skirting with the notion of love.

Why would someone only pretend at love? Very likely, there are forces working against this wind of love...forces in life that poison the good name, counteract all that is good. If the emotional tug of war is merely a game, the one really trying is going to get hurt.

Love may be a fanciful notion, but it is most assuredly not a game to be played.

Love has a way of slapping you in the face. We have felt love's gentle breeze and want more, so we observe, we take those slaps in the face...we turn the other cheek, and still the pain endures and the arrogant, self-righteous purveyor of pain continues on as if they are totally correct in their reprimanding behavior.

It's tough to fall in love with someone like this, yet we let down our guard and follow our hearts into the depths of hell. We open our hearts and arms to those who are reaching out to us and anticipate the same in

STH

kind. Folks warn us, 'you're gonna get hurt'...but we plow on, harvesting the winds of love and desire and oblivious that we are working alone.

It is completely natural for any human with a heart to open it when the right person comes along...or so we think 'the right person comes along.' The heart takes charge and has a way of leading over the head...caution to the wind, our heart is telling us things and the head doesn't listen.

Love really is blind...and deaf and dumb as well.

Things fall into place, folks fall in love all the time, and sometimes fall 'out of love' and go looking elsewhere for the love that has faded...sometimes before they are separated or divorced or before someone dies.

Sometimes they are of a faith that strictly forbids divorce and they continue to sleep in separate rooms, put up a good front at church and social events...they go to the wine and cheese tasting events at the country club and for all concerned they are just normal, married folks, still in love, long after the silver anniversary has tarnished and passed.

These are lonely hearts in search of some love that has left their home and heart. They find someone, someone who maybe has been through the same set of circumstances...two lost souls, if you will, one single and solitary, the other still married in name only, but longing to be loved.

STH

When these two star-crossed lovers meet and
discover their hearts are becoming one, the time shared
can bring unbounded happiness for both of them, most
of the time, not all the time, some of the time.

A magical force of wind blows into the souls and
new beginnings can be realized, that is, unless one
of the persons becomes afraid, unwilling to allow the
happiness to awaken them.

They pull back from their instinct and must rely on
the advices of a shrink to tell them what to do, or a padre
who is of the dark ages, not in tune with the times, to tell
their stories to.

Love becomes fleeting and there is no 'caution to the
wind.' They retreat to their comfort zone and the other
person is resigned to a cold wind...drifting and swirling
softly in a tired, aging heart, alone again, as they were
before this person came along.

Is it a greater sin to remain in an 'unloving marriage'
than it is to fall in love while still married, and then have
the courage and belief in one's self to move on with the
new love they have found?

Is it right to lean on prescription 'soul numbers' and
tranquilizers to shield a heart from accepting the reality
of falling in love...to numb the urges of powerful love
wanting to bloom once again in a life that is moving on
to the end of the road?

STH

It's all the rougher when one of the two opens up to a new adventure, openly and honestly, without having to ask the advices of anyone else...they are confident in their own beliefs that this is the path they want to walk. The other, seemingly just as committed and intelligent, is living a lie or they, too, would follow their heart.

Their hearts are guided by others and their own thoughts are tainted by the advice that their happiness is not something to go searching for. I suppose, then, that Will Shakespeare was indeed a fraud.

Brings to mind the book "Bridges of Madison County" and the way it brings out a love story, an infidelity if you will, of a pure and honest yearning on the part of one person, and the dynamic of another...a fateful encounter that burns so brightly for a short period, and then things get back to normal.

Or do things ever get back to normal after an encounter of unrealized love? The impact of love has a way of making daily life anything but normal. "All the lonely people, where do they all come from?" Father MacKenzie and Eleanor Rigby bear news of this unrequited love, as proclaimed by Lennon and McCartney.

No one runs away, no one really gets hurt. Little dramas like this go on every day in every little town in the country. There are times when a person's searching,

STH

one's desire to 'harness the wind' or at least build
a shelter to redirect it can be realized by another's
involvement.

Love has a way of blowing its own way, but
sometimes, just sometimes, you can work with someone
and perform the impossible. Sometimes the wind can
indeed be harnessed.

Only then can the forces of nature trump the forces of
man. Only then can love be realized and embraced.

Lots of 'only's' and that's life without regrets...live
each day to the fullest, don't be afraid to throw caution
to the wind, and let nature take its course.

======= 30 =======

Remembering
Jennings Scarborough

One of the mainstays of this column is remembering folks we grew up with, some who went on to live far away and yet we still keep in touch. Such was the case with Bobby Gallion and Jennings Scarborough, two wild and crazy guys who grew up in the Dublin area.

Bob is a regular reader of the Star and sent me this note recently. The best thing I could do is let his words tell the amazing story of the great friendship he and Jennings had.

Remembering Jennings

"Some may not be aware that Jennings was known by his middle name, Kelly, after he moved to California. Our mothers were 1st cousins and Jennings and I were 2nd cousins through the Webb family of Fawn Grove Pennsylvania. Our mothers grew up together and were very close. Jennings and I also grew up together, never living more than 5 miles apart.

Aside from my parents, Jennings' parents had more influence on my moral and ethical development than anyone, and I was enriched by my association with the Scarboroughs.

Jennings and I were classmates through elementary &
high school and we did a lot of crazy stuff together.

I recall when he had an old Hudson sedan that
he torched the top off of and one summer morning
Jennings, Delmer, Bob Ford & I were on our way to
school in it when the right rear wheel came off, hit a
utility pole and bounced over the electric wires just after
we passed a school bus.

Three of the lug nuts were still in the hubcap so the
three of us lifted the car while Jennings put the wheel
back on and we made it to school on time.

Then there was the time he strapped an 18 HP, 52
MPH Mercury outboard motor on a 4 X 8 ft sheet of
plywood with flotation pockets and we raced & jumped
small waves with it on Conowingo Lake.

He also built a glider with pontoons and flew it off
of the lake behind an inboard power boat. He water
skied bare foot and Jennings, his Dad and I were on
the bottom of a three-tiered water ski pyramid with his
sisters, Audrey & Rachel. We swam, sailed, water skied,
ice skated, ice sailed and had general good fun at the
Scarborough cottage on Broad Creek.

Jennings and I were in the Boy Scouts and we went
to summer camps and jamborees together. We also
danced to Benny Goodman at a scout dance in the Lord

STH

Baltimore Hotel (not together, we had dates). We also
went with the scouts on a two-week Naval Reserve cruise
to Nova Scotia on a Destroyer Escort (no dates).

A few years later, a bunch of us went dancing
to Glen Miller at the Starlight Ballroom in Hershey,
Pennsylvania. Jennings, Delmer, Bob Ford and I drove
up to Niagara Falls in '55 to see the ice jam and were
chased off the ice by a Reserve Deputy.

The Deputy told us there was 60 ft of diagonally
stacked ice sheets over 100 ft of water flowing 30 MPH.
He said if we slipped on one of those ice sheets we would
slide 60 feet into freezing water and over the falls. Like I
said, we did a lot of crazy stuff together.

Jennings flew F-86Hs in the Air National Guard
for about 6 months and one of the fun things he did
was fly to Maine and bring lobsters back in the ammo
magazines. He had placed in the top 2 or 3 in his
advanced flight training schools with the Air Guard so
the regular Air Force lured him to join with an offer to
fly anything he wanted and he selected F-102s or F-104s.

The Air force took months to process and while he
waited accumulated over 500 hours in National Guard
F-86 flight time to qualify for his solo cross-country
rating. As soon as he qualified, he hopscotched Air
Bases across the Northeast, down the Midwest and back
across the South to his home base in Baltimore.

STH

After his processing was finally complete, in typical
military fashion, the Air Force put him in B-52s flying
bombing missions in the Vietnam War. The thought
of collateral injury and death of innocent civilians,
women and children soon began to wear on Jennings'
sensibilities and he resigned his commission as soon as
he satisfied his commitment to the Air Force.

After resigning from the Air Force, he trained in a
Lear Jet as a civilian occupation back up and applied for
major airline pilot positions. His first wife, Kate, another
couple and Carol & I flew with him on his final check
ride to Salt Lake City for dinner and we stayed overnight
at his ski lodge in Park City.

We did touch and goes, tight turns, stalls and engine
out takeoffs as part of the check ride. The girls got off
after the first tight turn but I wouldn't have missed the
other maneuvers for anything. Quite a ride and the last
crazy thing we did together.

Jennings was also an avid bird watcher and while
flying showed me how to spot birds riding thermals.
We steered to join the birds in a spiral altitude gain
to several thousand feet where we ran out of lift. He
pushed over into a steep dive reaching about 120 MPH
when he pulled up into a full loop.

The weight of the helmet with the G-force of the loop
pulled my chin down on my chest and I could not pull it
up to see what was happening. He just laughed, caught
another thermal and headed back to the air strip. After

we landed, he told me it was the first time he had looped this glider. We must have stimulated a daring in each other.

We maintained casual contact over the years, spent several weekends together, traveled to the Central California Coast and Mexico together with our wives, visited, emailed and talked on the phone occasionally.

When my wife was in the hospital and Jennings had a layover at the LA airport, I picked him up on my motorcycle and took him to visit her. He thought my motorcycle was fun but I thought his flying was much more fun. Jennings had a full life and suffered a terrible illness. I will miss him greatly.   -- Bob.

Thank you Bob for this excellent remembrance of a guy many in this area knew. A recollection of mine was when Jennings bought a new Austin-Healey 3000 convertible sports car. It was a beautiful, cream colored baby with red leather interior. I saw it and smelled it... wow! Never had seen a spiffy car like that in my life...

So Jennings says, 'Do you want to take it for a spin?'... Double Wow!! He showed me the gearing, we both strapped in and headed out from Reuben's down to Aldino Airpark and the back roads for a great thrill...not many folks would do that for a younger guy. Jennings did, and I'll never forget it.

STH

It's sad when someone you remember from years ago suddenly is back in your thoughts like Jennings, who suffered losses that would break many men. His wife Mary gave all she could and surely he felt her love when his struggles began.

========= 30 =========

Coming Around, Going Around

Like so many of my friends nearly my age, I see lots of grandparents raising their own grandkids. Just when things are looking up for grandma and grandpa, with good health and a little stashed away from years of work and sacrifice, the time comes where they can spend the years they have left enjoying each other's company. Then, for whatever reason one of the kids falls apart and the little ones are in jeopardy.

They pitch in and do what's right and take in the grandchild or grandchildren...to raise them right...to do it all over, so to speak. You see a pal watching a football game at the same high school he once played football for...he watched his son play football, now he's watching his grandson play football. His grandson lives with grand pop and grand mom.

He's proud of his grandson...he tells me I should come see him play, I do...the kid is good. But it's a bit tougher to sit in the stands for a second or third generation as sole provider for the kid, no matter how much love you have for what you're doing.

A lot of our kids moved out to 'find themselves' and got apartments with their friends and with even a low-paying job they could afford the rent and groceries and pay the bills. Sometimes, for whatever reason, it just didn't work out and they ended up having to move home for awhile so that mom and dad could help them make ends meet.

Others of us had children who worked jobs and went to school, but somehow they just couldn't make it on their own. These kids had plans and were living in a transitional state...the security of home and the promise of a future.

Some a little younger than me have kids, they grow up, go to school, get a job, get married, get hooked on drugs, wreck their lives and then announce , "I'm moving back home, mom."

Yes, it can happen just when the house is literally getting bigger, with that guest room now ready for a guest or two when there's a class reunion or some mutual pal passes on and an old acquaintance travels back home for the memorial service. For the most part, it's just mom and pop...maybe for a couple years, maybe not.

Sometimes, the kid's a simple screw up, can't keep a job, doesn't like real work, or is on drugs and just can't get their stuff together. So they come home, back to the same room even. It's sad.

Some don't even offer to pay a little for food, sort of 'to help mom and pop out.' I know these parents. I visit with them from time to time. I see the slug sitting in front of the TV. and I bite my tongue. Why? Because it irks me to see good parents, who are also good friends,

STH

being taken for granted by a shiftless slacker. The term today is 'enabler'...and that's what the parents are called just for doing what they feel they must do, because after all, it's 'their kid.'

The screwed up kid story is all too real. Everyone these days seems to know of a pal who has a kid lost in the fog of what we used to call just growing up.

Of course, there are also the good kids who have to come back home for a while, just because the economy is so harsh, and getting by on your own is a tough thing to do. These days, a transition stage can last for years.

For those parents reaching out to help their kids, good story or sad story, raising grandkids or relinquishing their own privacy, we should tip a hat and show our kindness.

That's a noble thing to do...to continue on in spite of old age, frailties and loss of income, to still find a way to care for someone, to reach out and give of ourselves at a time when we should be enjoying the sunsets of our lives.

For those helping out the kids in that transitional stage, I hope the transition is short lived, because making your own way is, well, the right way. Yet, for those having to reach out and help out the kids who are struggling with life and who appear to 'allow' mom and dad to take care of them, my heart goes out to you. We

STH

all know folks like this, and we count our blessings that we are not in that boat. Who knows, if we were there we might very well do exactly the same thing.

These thoughts raced through my mind when at the age of 73 I was faced with a situation where I would need help after living alone for lots of years. Off and on, after divorce, I've lived with some fine women, truly. For various reasons not relevant here I did not re-marry, and some of the relationships drifted apart. Recalling it takes 'two to tango'...no one to bless, no one to blame... just life going on.

The situation was this. After years of knee injuries, repeated arthroscopic surgeries, cortisone shots and loss of more and more mobility I had to decide to undergo major surgery, in my case, double knee replacements. Fine...it got to that point and after three opinions, maybe five, I chose the surgeon and figured I would be home after maybe 4 or 5 days in hospital.

I had everything mapped out. My pals could ride over and check on the dogs and I would be fine in short order. I could sit on my fanny and get up and down the stairs to the bedroom and life would be back to normal in a matter of weeks.

Well, being in denial with major surgery is the way I chose to deal with things. Thankfully, my son and daughter had more realistic concerns. When the surgeries were done and I was able to begin rehab, the

STH

doctor told me I would be wise to go to another hospital for a couple of weeks of physical therapy at least, then maybe get home.

That's when something unheard of occurred. My son and daughter offered me their homes to further recuperate and do rehab in. At first I resisted, thinking, unwisely that I could do all of this recovery on my own. They persisted and I gained a better grip on the severity of the situation, agreeing to go to my son's home after my release from hospital.

I spent three weeks living with my son, seeing his day to day life, his pals, his working schedule, his humor, his cooking and I was able to do all this with two of my three pups...Little Dude and Chester were there with me, at my son's, with his pup, Roxy.

It was a twist you might say. When does a parent come to live with their offspring? Sure, in the old days, it was commonplace for a parent to be living with a son or daughter. Not so as much these days...us oldsters get shipped to nursing homes or other places of that ilk.

So it came to be that my time with Sam, with many days of care by Mina, who came to spell Sam when he was working, unfolded in a most amazing way. They were 'caring' for me, taking care of this guy who thought he was invincible...and to be honest, it was a richly rewarding experience, a rarity these days, and a precious insight into a younger world.

STH

More on this later, for now, I'm back home at Rustica....with all three of my pups and lots of friends helping me out in oh so many ways. Truly, there is a new and beautiful bond with those kids I helped raise with a good wife...and it took major surgery to really find out what a good job we did, and to see firsthand the rewards of good parenting.

========= 30 =========

Lost and Found

Have you ever lost something that really meant a lot to you? Have you searched high and low and not found what you're looking for? Have you lost it forever? Retraced your steps from the last time you had whatever it was you lost in the hopes it would appear? Maybe you found it years later, in a place where it had sat unnoticed?

We've all lost 'things' and 'loves' in life...one way or another. If you're Scots-Irish, the sentimental attachment to little things goes deep and far into our psyches. A little item from the past family I've come from means more than gold. A little green tool box, made 100 years ago that my great-grandfather, Stockton Whiteside Holden used when he was an undertaker in Delta is here lending support whenever I see it.

The attachment is of course a link to my heritage and the folks who came before me. But why certain things? What makes it special? Who knows...it's just the way it is.

So it came to pass the other day I lost a gold signet ring that was my high school graduation present from my dad...it was hand-lettered by a jeweler in Baltimore, but more on that later.

STH

Due to weight loss from the surgeries a while back, my fingers are thinner, the ring slipped off and so began this little adventure. Read on and I'll tell you the outcome...as I told it to my son and a few close friends of mine.

"You are all special to me...so very special, in so many ways...of course my son...but friends too, reach a level as a 'son' or 'brother'...to you I write this from the heart tonight...

"Sammy...you remember so many years ago, I lost a little Buck Knife...and I asked you to ride with me to the Joppa-Magnolia fire hall the day after I shot a wedding reception there...it was at least 15 hours after my work was done, and I went to where my car was parked and walked around...you remember that day...and I found, on that parking lot the little Buck Knife...pristine, not damaged by a car...after all the cars on the lot had left... there it was...and I told you to 'just believe'...your Dad could do it...

"Holly...one day working on the tractor you lost a couple of little screws...in all that dirt and debris...and I said I'd look...I could find it...I wasn't wrong, was I?....you couldn't believe it when I found those little screws...that were almost invisible...

"Pat...you came so quick today, to help me find my gold signet ring that my dad bought for me in 1957...he knew the jeweler in Baltimore...Norman Meddinger... an 'old world' craftsman who allowed me to be back in

STH

his work area and let me watch as he crafted my initials
'STH'...free-hand in script...freehand!!! That ring later
became my wedding band....Mr. Meddinger made a
ladies model, with the exact same script for Ann and we
eloped. We could not wear actual wedding bands...our
parents were not in favor of our love and union...so the
ring again came into play as Ann put it on my finger that
afternoon in 1963, September 19th.

"Not sure whatever became of Ann's ring...it doesn't
matter now...anymore....

"A few years ago, for some reason I dug out the signet
ring, well worn and put it on...and it meant so much to
me to wear it again, and be part of what it stood for at
least to me...sentimental?...sure...

"So it was tough after Sammy left the other day and
I could not find the ring...but I knew I could find it...
somehow I just felt once again I could find something
precious that was lost. Today, logically thinking the ring
may have slipped off on the Wheel Horse when I went
down to the pond to see Sam...and mowed some along
the way...Holly's new blades didn't need to be tested
in the rough and rocky hillside...so I raised the deck to
protect them...maybe that's when the ring slipped off my
smaller fingers.

"Holly came over and walked the path...Pat and
I walked the path...and Holly was gonna get a metal
detector to search. "So it was, just a few minutes ago, I
felt the urge to grab the walking stick and walk again...

STH

along the path to the pond. The grass was wet, shiny
and slick. Good thing I had my stick. I felt safer and
Sam and everyone else would've gotten on me. Anyway,
I poked along and why, I can't tell you...I stopped just
south of the ground hog vent hole about a quarter of
the way to the pond...and there, in the clover, was my
ring...the ring that means more than it should and you
may think I'm nuts for feeling the way I do about some
things...but that's just the way it is...the way I am...and I
make no apologies, nor seek no accolades for what I am
and what I do.

With a ring of truth. Photo by Todd Holden.

"But never, ever doubt my intuition...it's real, it's
here, it's part of me...and the ring is where it's supposed
to be tonight...and I am so grateful...I wanted to share
this with the ones I love." I've said it before...I'll say it
again...'I'm a lucky guy.'

========= 30 =========

STH

Conscience Comes Creeping In

"They say everything can be replaced
They say every distance is not near
So I remember every face
Of every man who put me here"

These words, written by Robert Zimmerman in 1967
bring many thoughts of conscience to bear in mind...my
mind, if you will. For myself, I can't bear to hear or see
someone being wrongly accused of anything. No matter
what. You know what I mean, someone who didn't do
something that they are being accused of doing.

"I see my light come shinin'
From the west down to the east
Any day now, any day now
I shall be released"

There are times when a film is so full of a story of
someone being treated unfairly, or wrongly, that at first
it captivates my imagination, then, as the story unfolds
and the wrong isn't 'righted' ...a sickening feeling comes
over me. Films such as 'Shawshank Redemption' come
to mind. In life, there are folks in prison for something
they did not do. What a terrible life they have to live,
not only behind bars for something they didn't do, but
knowing they didn't do it and trying to wrestle that
dilemma daily.

STH

"They say every man needs protection
They say that every man must fall
Yet I swear I see my reflection
Somewhere so high above this wall"

There once was a lady in town who always 'told the news' to anyone who came in her store...a store that I patronized often for her wares. Often, she could be found holding court, relating some news of the day with her twist...after all, this was a small town and local news came by word of mouth.'

So one day I overhear her telling a tale about someone, a hurtful tale because for a fact I knew she was not getting the story straight. I listened to her misspeak until I could take no more.

"Excuse me," I said amidst the folks listening, "that's just not the way it happened...you've got the story all wrong."

Well, the look I got was as though I had blasphemed the chosen one. This was indeed her turf, but I just had to speak up in defense of someone being wrongly accused, tried and convicted by the high court of this lady of words.

"I see my light come shinin'
From the west down to the east
Any day now, any day now
I shall be released"

   She said back to me in a firm voice, "Well, since you
know more than I do, why don't you tell us all your
version?"

   "Well then, since there are others here to verify what
I'm about to say, I know you can't get it screwed up
like you did the first time. Then I told the truth of the
matter, objectively but truthfully. She was silent...she
didn't like being corrected. Sorry, didn't mean to offend
her, but it was wrong what she was doing and things just
had to be set straight.

   We've all done this at one time or another. We find
that we have to speak up to deliver the facts, especially
when it defends someone who can't defend themselves.
Those standing, listening, kinda looked at me as an
authority of some sort, which I am not. Never was my
intention to take the shop owner's place and spread
news, just set things right.

   Still, even now, something misinformed comes my
way, seems a duty to right it. When I wrote for *The Aegis*,
it was a great newspaper...we got it right, always in the
best interest of the readers. Folks used to call the paper,
'the gospel according to St. John' ...referring to then
editor John D. Worthington, Jr.

> "Now yonder stands a man in this lonely crowd
> A man who swears he's not to blame
> All day long I hear him shouting so loud
> Just crying out that he was framed"

STH

I worked for the newspaper from 1966 to 1972...seems like longer, but that was the term of my apprenticeship in the world of photo-journalism. I was never in the clique in high school, those who did the yearbook or the school newspaper.

In college, I was overwhelmed at the big University of Maryland, College Park...I just read a lot, studied Hemingway, James, Shelley, Keats and Byron. Many of their themes were of folks wrongly accused of things... the groundwork was being laid.

> "I see my light come shinin'
> From the west down to the east
> Any day now, any day now
> I shall be released"

Not that any of my life story means anything now, in the present. Maybe just because all these years have helped me understand folks better all the time, to love the ones who are straight and true, respect my elders who offer wisdom in small packages and to pass that along as they have to me, so I do for the readers of these columns.

No big thing. You'd do it too. Because it's the right thing to do...and sometimes, you just do what you gotta do.

========= 30 =========

Just What I Need

When I was much younger and able to speed through the challenges life threw at me, there wasn't a whole lot I needed other than my own stamina and drive. I loved living and the work I did. That means a lot to enjoy your livelihood; otherwise, you're just punching the clock. I have always worked hard and gotten through by counting on myself, first and foremost.

Of course, no man is an island and I couldn't have gotten through this world without help from friends, family, acquaintances both business and personal, decent eating establishments, and a relaxing tavern or two to unwind in. I've enjoyed the ride so far and thankful for those I've counted on.

Whatever your path, there are just a few things that you need. Let me tell you, based on my experiences and in my humble opinion, there are two things you must have to get through life...a good doctor and a good mechanic. There are many perks in life that come our way, but to be honest these are two of the essentials.

An ailment not tended to will likely fester and get worse, and a smooth ride has more to do with the mechanic who keeps the engine humming than the model you drive.

STH

My first ride was a Volkswagen Beetle. Matter of
fact, I have owned more than a few of these Beetles,
even a Volkswagen Van and later on a diesel Rabbit. All
of these cars were serviced by the best, Donald Hyson
of Fawn Grove. Mr. Hyson surely knew his stuff and I
could always count on him to keep my little VWs going.

Back then, the garage and the gasoline service were
one and the same and you could always stop and say hi
to the mechanic when you pulled in for a fill-up.

Remember when you would pull up to the service
pump and the young kid would run out to your car
asking if you wanted regular or high test? After getting
the pump going, the kid would check under the hood,
wipe around the hood ornament area when he shut the
hood, and wash the windows...all with a thank you.
Well, some of you may remember.

A long time has passed since those days and now
the vehicles are all driven by computers. My Expedition
conked out on me the other day while I was driving and
when I took it in to the shop the fix was in rebooting
the computer. A lot of folks get viruses on their home
computer; I sure hope I don't get one under my hood.
The man who fixed it was none other than George
Donhauser who runs Del Haven Service. The man is
honest, efficient, fair, prompt for appointments, and uses
good common sense. He's just the best and I hope he
doesn't retire or go out of business before I stop driving
altogether.

STH

Now, as far as a good doctor...well, it's just like having a good mechanic. You put your trust in the person wielding the tools of trade and expect that they will keep you out of harm's way. I've always been lucky to have a good doctor to take care of me.

Far and away, the best doc in town for many years was Dr. Heuman. He tidied up many cuts and injuries and kept me going. My dad would take me in when I had a mishap, and he would get out the ammonia bottle just in case I passed out once he started the stitching... he and his able assistant, Marguerette Ward, were my saviors for many years. When I was seriously hurt, Doc Heuman would take care of me in the truest sense of the word caring. There was just no one else like him.

As I've gotten older and witnessed the extreme change in what we call health care, I have also nurtured new ailments like the knees, the heart, and other principle body parts you just can't do without. Habern Freeman has cured many of my back and neck ailments and is absolutely the best when it comes to aches and pain and overall soreness.

For the more delicate situation of keeping my heart in working order, I have to thank Dr. Joseph Reinhardt for diagnosing me to a 'T' and always doing the right thing. You won't find many heart doctors like him...ask around and just about everyone will sing his praises. Fortunately, each one of the specialists I've encountered has put up with me, patched me up, kept me going, and generally kept me up and running as the years mount up.

Thus, a good mechanic for the car and a good mechanic for me are more than just good words to live by, or die by...they're just what I need.

========= 30 =========

Lemme Tell Ya

How many times, so I'm told, do I chat with someone and start off by saying, "I tell you what." Hadn't paid much attention, but I'm told it's not a fake line or plain old BS, rather it comes across as the real deal, no bull, straight arrow.

A shorter version, said in haste or possibly stressing more urgency when issuing a statement, one might use 'Tell you what,' as if declaring the answer to some long, lost question of big significance. "Lemme tell ya" also fits in with this item.

Suffice to say, aside from the good-natured pokin' fun or flat out jawin' a bit, I don't BS and what you're going to get out of me is indeed a straight shot. Fact is, I've been around the block enough times and heard my share of folks blowing their own horn or flat out making stuff up long enough to know that if you don't tell it straight, well, you're just never gonna be taken seriously.

Of course, I don't live or die by what others think... then again, if I do have something worthwhile to say I would rather be taken seriously. When the time comes, it's good to know that you never pulled a leg that didn't deserve it...and telling it like it is sure beats telling a lie.

STH

Lemme tell ya...

It's a crying shame to go down the road only to have
someone barrel past you or maybe just cut you off to get
where they're going. I've always paid attention to the
speed limits and figure the folks who designed the roads
knew what they were doing with how fast you ought to
go. For the most part, I take my time and enjoy the ride.
Sadly, there's a ton of folks out there who don't care a bit
about anyone around them and go zooming in and out of
lanes thinking only of themselves.

Believe me, it doesn't hurt to slow down and watch
out for someone who may be trying to get out on the
road, switch lanes, or make a turn. If we took the time
to watch out for the other guy and maybe drive with a
little more friendliness, perhaps the traffic would flow
a little better. With all the cars and trucks on the road,
we won't fix all the congestion or road rage, but we sure
might improve the ride.

Lemme tell ya...

The saddest part about growing older as an American
is to see our young children so mixed up and confused.
Worst of all are those who simply come unglued and
resort to shooting and violence as a way to get some
attention. Many other young adults are wandering
aimlessly with no sense of responsibility, no real interest
in achieving a goal or being accountable.

STH

Being a kid today is probably a lot harder, but unless we can lend a hand soon we won't have many children left to grow into adults and carry on where we leave off. Our country will only be as good as what we can nurture and giving up on the future is just plain unforgiving.

Lemme tell ya...

There's a lot of folks who read *The Star*, and lots of them like to read this column, and that's a blessing. I've said it before–the kind words, and even sometimes critical words mean a lot to me. It means you care enough to buy the paper, to read it and to take the time to make a comment to others.

Let me tell you, in this almost archaic way of communication, from the comments I get, from the folks who stop me here, there and everywhere, these stories, this column is both rewarding and relevant. There are stories of simple life and hard truth...of wonderful people and a few n'er do wells...of the land we are stewards of and the creatures who coexist beside us, or in spite of us as it goes sometimes.

We are being reminded of the same things, things that once were so prevalent and today are not. We grow and change from year to year, but memories are the treasures we are allowed to look back on from time to time.

STH

When someone at the table or in the car says, "Lemme tell ya..." usually it's a good thing, sometimes we've heard it before, and that's o.k.

========= 30 =========

An Open Book

H ow's Dude? Those were the first words from Tom Moore when he walked into the dining room of Taylor Haus where The Delta Crew had gathered to celebrate Millie "Mother Superior" Hunt's 95th birthday.

Lord Nelson, better known as Dude. Photo by Sam Holden.

For sure, this day was the day, 95 years ago, lovely Millie was born to Mr. and Mrs. Lane Whitaker. At the table, it was a joyous time and we were all relating stories of growing up in Delta and hanging out at the Hunt house and down at Addie Holden's for little circuses, puppet shows and games of chance and aerial acrobatics by a blind-folded Lane Hall in a Tarzan loin cloth.

Folks from other tables are coming over to acknowledge father time and the battle he's had with Millie, who just won't submit to age either physically or mentally...she just stays young at heart thanks to her vigorous constitution and happy outlook on life. I'm sure her daughter, Linda Lane Henry, has a lot to do with it too.

STH

So, in the midst of this celebration, in walks Tom Moore, he spots me and the first thing out of his mouth is, "How's Little Dude?"

Really, it's like the first time someone says to you, "Hi, are you little Johnny's dad?" You know what I mean, you're recognized not for who you are, but who your son or daughter is.

This was a first for me, not that I haven't been spotted by someone who says, "Are you Mina's dad?" or "Was Gwynne Holden your dad?" It's a good feeling for all of us when this happens, for sure...but to be recognized as the 'pal' of Little Dude? C'mon!

So Tom ambles over to the party table, I introduce him all around and he sits on my knee, like a kid on Santa's lap at Christmastime and proceeds to ask about The Dude...he knows more about my pup than most folks. He knows that Dude came from the farm of Daniel Lapp and now Daniel doesn't have any more Jack Russell's.

Matter of fact, Daniel called me a year ago to ask if I was breeding Dude, but alas, to keep Dude home and safe here at Rustica, I had to have him 'clipped' so unfortunately, there will be no 'Little Little Dudes' and that's a bummer, because he is one in a million all around as dogs go.

STH

After catching up on the Dude, Tom wished Millie another 'Happy Birthday' and headed out. Believe you me, it just struck me funny, how folks relate and recall what they read in The Star and how my life is an open book in so many ways.

A lady I was dating said to me years ago, "You know, I know your heart was broken and you'll never love like you did again." It was sad to hear that from such a nice lady, but in the end, likely it is true. She knew a lot about me from the columns I had written.

It's all good to share, as this comment from Steeleye Sloan sums up, regarding the Delta Crew and our adventures...

"What a fun time we had yesterday! Aren't you glad you had the idea of starting these Delta Crew gatherings? I believe everybody - and I mean everybody within earshot - at Taylor Haus had a good time. I suppose we're actually a bit of an historical club. Cheers!"

There is history, we make it each and every day, especially if we have the heart and soul and spirit of folks from Delta like Millie Hunt and many others.

This all may sound odd to some of you, not all of you, but some of you, and needs sharing. Today, as I headed out to run errands, it was raining, so Dude and Frisco are relegated to the sun space, plenty of room to stretch out, sleep, whatever they want. It's overcast, so it won't get too hot for them. They have plenty of water.

STH

As I gather up my stuff, I turn and look at the two pups. Frisco is laying down on the big carpet by the sliding door, content, but watching my every move.

Dude is sitting as close to the slider into the living room as he can, so forlorn, looking right at me, as if to say, "Hey buddy, I'm supposed to go for a ride with you." Can't do that today because I'm riding with Keith the locksmith and there's little room in the cab for Dude.

There is a pain when we have to leave someone we love. Humans feel the twinge of pain kissing a loved one good bye, if only for a few hours or days. We are connected to other beings in ways beyond description.

I am connected to my roommates, my companions here at Rustica...the older pup, Frisco, understands and takes it in stride, although she is a lover of the long rides to Delta and other spots north of town. Dude is more of a personal trainer for me, he knows before I act what the next scene is to be. Today, he still sits as I write this scribble, and I feel bad leaving him behind. What would become of the two pups if I didn't come back?

Don't know why but that's the way it is when you love a pup and the pups love you all the more. I promise, when I get back we will go for a ride, somewhere, doesn't matter where, and we will be content this rainy day.

========= 30 =========

STH

The Waiting Is Over

On Saturday, March 12, at 8:30 pm, there was a reunion in heaven. Whitey finally caught up with Punky...they were together again, renewing their vows, among old pals, family and friends.

The first time, it was November 7, 1942, when Eugene married his sweetheart and it lasted until May 19, 2008, when Punky passed on. In his heart, Whitey was still married to the woman he adored.

I don't think Whitey ever recovered from this loss... living alone, doing the chores you once both did together is a tough row to hoe, and those of us who know Whitey, know his heart just wasn't into living without Punky, but he carried on doing the best he could.

On a visit before Punky died, Whitey was sitting at the kitchen table when I walked in, but Punky was nowhere in sight. Before we said much, he said he'd have to get Punky 'up.' I said, "No, don't do that, don't bother her. Let her rest."

"Toddy, if she finds out you were here and I didn't tell her, I'll catch all kinds of hell." I'm not one to cause problems for a pal, so I told him to go ahead.

STH

Eugene 'Whitey' Probst (left) and his brother John Probst. Whitey
and Punky are together again. Photo by Todd Holden.

He loved Wendy's and no matter when I came to
visit, it was lunchtime. I've shared coffee and food with
Whitey many times over the years.

He told me he loved the smell of perfume on girls and
wished he'd been born a day later than 2/21/22, cause he
could share the day with George Washington. He liked
Holstein cattle as much as cats, peafowl, canada geese
and ducks.

Whitey told me of the time he met my dad...after
whistling at my Mom who was driving a nifty red 1949
Willy's Jeepster convertible.

STH

"Did you whistle at my wife?" questioned my dad.

"I whistled, but I didn't know it was your wife," replied Whitey.

"Well, every time you see her, you whistle at her, okay?"

"I can do that," Whitey said and he and dad were friends from then on. That was 1953.

Or the time he and John went to Delaware Park and Whitey picked the $10 winner and it was John's horse, although John hadn't told him it was his until they got to the winner's circle for a photograph.

The stories Whitey told of using a shovel or a rake to chase off hooligans who were going to paint his barn or sly hunters who came in to hunt. Punky would save 'Arizona Highways' magazines for me and I would save newspapers for her, for peahen bedding.

Whitey was sharp as a tack right to the end. He asked me what crop I was putting in this year, then asked me for something to spit his tobacco juice in...that was a tough one, but I did it.

I will still turn into his lane from habit. The lane was always smooth, the door always unlocked with Whitey sitting erect at the table.

STH

Things are changed with his passing for many of
us. He was a good man, a good friend, and now he and
Punky are together again. After all, they mated for life
and Whitey showed his colors long ago.

========= 30 =========

Scott Creek...From a Distance

R ecently I visited some families living very close
to Bunker Hill Road along Scott Creek, on the
north side of Delta. More folks know this once pristine
area as a 'convenient dumping place' to drop off the
old, flea-ridden sofa or the washing machine that took
a dump just before the holidays. It's just not the right
thing to do, to take stuff that could easily go elsewhere
and nonchalantly load it up in the pick-up and drive over
to Bunker Hill Road, making sure the coast is clear, and
passing the shiny new signs that warn 'dumpers' of a
$1,000 fine for littering. But hell, you have to catch them
to fine them.

The old system of walking down the embankment
and going through some of the trash in hopes of finding
a name, address...anything to link that particular trash
heap with the person to whom it belonged...could
provide some good detective work.

That doesn't necessarily mean it's the person who
dumped it, but it's a start in deterring the dumping. I
urge anyone reading this to keep in mind that I honestly
don't think we're dealing with a lot of nasty folks who
use this tranquil area for their trash. My guess would be
it's only a few daring folks who continue to litter along
Scott Creek.

STH

Three of the people I met with recently said it's
still a problem. One lady who was walking her beagle
along the road as I approached her said it's still bad,
and she carries a cell phone with her in case she comes
upon someone littering. She said the roadway was
clearer now, but that could change any time. She lives
on Watson Road and takes daily walks with her dog
along Bunker Hill. She couldn't pick a more pristine
area for a healthy walk with her dog. This is what Scott
Creek is all about, a place of beauty in nature, where a
very historic wooden trestle built for the Maryland and
Pennsylvania Railroad many years ago still stands.

It's in disrepair now, long overlooked and ignored
by everyone, but not the tall sycamore trees and poplar
and oak that have fallen across the roadbed. Still, there's
a subtle beauty of this structure, still standing, but
lingering in old age and frailty.

Other towns spend tons of money to 'recreate' a place
like Delta already has. Big shots came and went to town
meetings to speak of a trail similar to the Ma and Pa
Trail in Harford County.

I listened to the proponents and the opponents and
then the axe fell when the estimated costs of such a
project in Delta were discussed. On top of the current
state of affairs for many working folks, being eaten alive
by taxes, the high cost of living and health care, the price
tag of replenishing nature fell on deaf ears, including
mine.

STH

The plan didn't have the mojo of the existing Bunker Hill Road stretch along Scott Creek. There are just no reasons why this meandering trail couldn't become a gemstone of Delta. If you don't believe me, visit the road and see for yourself. Looking closely out over the side of the road one will see the tons of trash, but if you are in the car and just driving by, you see the beauty only, and that's a good thing, although it might mislead some people to think there is no problem there.

There is, but it's not unsolvable. Another resident nearby said it's a disgrace to have the trash so close to a relic of Delta's history, tied in with the railroad that used to run from Baltimore to York, with spurs all along the way for produce, fuel, and milk.

More of you are aware of the problem, and again, I don't think we're in as bad a shape as we could be. Some of the roads that are still unpaved in both York County and Harford County are sadly also used to dump what folks don't want.

If more people used Bunker Hill Road, there would be less chance of someone using it for dumping. Maybe it's asking too much from our younger readers to use this little, rough road every now and then when they're on their way home, just to bring a little more awareness when it's dark outside.

STH

This is just a thought, and maybe you have a better one to keep this idea alive and well and doing some good. We have "Save The Rocks" out there, doing a job to keep a pristine natural area free from 'over doing good doers' like the federal government.

We aren't that deep in bureaucracy yet with Scott Creek, we have the power and control to do what is best without 'uncle' breathing down our necks. It's an opportunity to do some good the old fashioned way... seeing a problem, taking some action to solve the problem and hopefully eliminate it. Then, we'd all have something that has grown into something more for everyone's benefit.

Think about it, now an eyesore, tomorrow and beyond a beautiful place for everyone, even the reformed litterers, to enjoy, to take pictures, to hike, walk and escape the routine without going to a health club or the treadmill in the basement. The best notion, too, is that of the townspeople of Delta getting together to solve the problem and make things better...that's the ticket.

========= 30 =========

None of Us Know

"thinking of a couple pals who are short on time...none of us know how long we've got...we don't want to know really, just get through another day as best we can and love a lot along the way..."

The author and Willard Pardew. Photo by Sam Holden.

H e was a young man, who traveled the country by car and thumb. The 'ankle express' was his sole means of transportation many times and he met a lot of different folks along the way. He asked me to ride with him twice on long, long rides, from my home near Bel Air to Prince Rupert, British Columbia.

STH

They were enlightening rides since the only real trips or vacations up till then were with family to tourist places staying in motels and stopping often. The family trips were always special and make for precious memories, but the rides with Will were different.

Just you and a buddy out on the open road with the landscape all around and no strings attached. They were slow and easy rides taking in the towns and small talk at cafes owned by mom and pop, who recommended the meat loaf and homemade apple pie.

Now, Will knew his mom, Zella Pardew, read a lot all through her life. She read everything Zane Grey had written. She liked westerns and tales of the west. Ultimately, she settled in Arizona to live out her years after a life of hard work and raising a big family pretty much by herself and her oldest daughter.

Back then, the oldest children accepted the job of helping raise the family. That kind of helped to really define a family, which is sorely missed today with our modern lifestyles. That aside, folks were resilient then in a quiet, accepting way.

So on one of his rides west to seek work and adventure, Will decided to do something a little different. He asked his mom to ride with him, as she had done many times. They traveled well together. A mom and son, both adventuresome and on the road again.

STH

Site of the Zane Grey cabin, in Arizona. Photographer unknown.

When they reached Arizona, Will had planned a surprise...he wanted to do something special for his mom. So it came to be, a ride to the cabin where Zane Grey wrote.

Located near Kohl's Ranch just beneath the Mogollon Rim, burnt in a lightning-initiated forest fire in June 1990, Zane Grey stayed here several weeks at a time off and on from 1923-1930. The cabin was at one time on the national registry.

So it was that Will took his mom, Zella, to the site of where many books no doubt took shape. How many of us have traveled with our moms to a place set deep in her memory? Knowing Will as a close friend and sharing those rides with him helps me appreciate it all

STH

the more, but...just imagine the close connection with someone, whether it's your mom or an acquaintance, and sharing an adventure.

Those rides or cruises are precious. All we have to do is 'do them'...just two people bringing the landscape and scenery into the front seat of their vehicle, sharing the experience with conversation, laughter, and meaning.

From there, it just gets better. There is a closer connection with your fellow passenger and whatever is happening in the town doesn't matter too much.

When times are open its nice to let some ideas flow allowing for adventures to happen with the ones we love and hold dear. We never know if we'll get the chance again.

 30

Words of Wisdom Recalled

N otable sometimes for the turn of phrase and other times the significance is more how it marked the moment, words of wisdom seem to carry us through life. We may have read them in a book or just heard them in conversation, but these idioms form the backbone of our conscious thought and allow us to understand perhaps a bit more of this world we live in.

A cup of joe and some wisdom. Photo by Todd Holden.

Take, for example, the following.

"I've never killed a man, but I've read many an obituary with a great deal of satisfaction.

"If you don't read the newspaper, you are uninformed; if you do read the newspaper, you are misinformed.

"If voting made any difference they wouldn't let us do it.

"The man who does not read good books has no advantage over the man who can't read them."

Each of these comments is so very true in their own way. The first quote reminded me of an old friend, who was in the car business. He bought and sold more cars around these parts than anyone I know of.

One sad day when he was nearing the end of his life he said if he had it to do over again, when he got the bad diagnosis and dismal prognosis, he said he wanted to get a gun and take care of two big crooks who did him wrong over the years.

His thinking was, I don't have long to live and I'm gonna take these two bums out before I go. "So, I'm arrested, possibly convicted if none of the jury knew of the two crooks I took care of, and sent to prison to live out what little time I have left."

When I had the honor of being asked by his family to do the eulogy for his memorial service, I did not mention this.

Sadly, when it comes to some of the bigger news sources, including TV and hard copy, the second comment (being misinformed) is often the case, in these days of lop-sided reporting and bias and slant and spin. Some of our local online papers are guilty of this too. Can't say that it applies to this very paper as I've never seen anything with a slant to it.

There is much comfort from quotations, be they from the Bible or the many folks who've been published. Good quotes come as well from the everyday folks we

STH

know. Mostly, the ones that stuck with me came from
the adults I knew as a kid. They would always have an
observation that just summed things up...and made you
think at the same time.

Winfield Mitchell had me out crabbing one day and
he wanted to check his turtle traps along Bush River. We
made for land and he hopped out of his boat, me not far
behind.

It was dense along the wood margin, very hard to see
much farther than 50 yards to be honest. He came back
and I mentioned the denseness to him. Winfield turned
and said, "Todd, this is where the owl lost sight of the
hare."

Point on vision well made, well spoken and never
forgotten. He was a remarkable man who taught me
ever so much about things rarely found in books. As my
years wander on I often impart some of these words of
wisdom that men like Winfield Mitchell, Wilson Ford,
Ellis Porter and Bill Kunkel have passed along to me.

It's part of the deal we make when we are born, to
be 'in the game' as long as we can and pass along things
that helped us so much, in the hope that they help
others. It's all totaled up when the deal goes down. I'm
still listening and reading words of wisdom anywhere
I can find them and sharing whenever I can. I'm still
living by the maxims even if my memory can't recall
them as easily.

STH

Has anybody seen my love? I don't know, just never know when we run into someone we haven't seen in a while, there's a tight connection to our hearts. Time and space vary in degrees of anticipation and anxiety when we by chance run into someone from long ago and far away.

Reckon that's the way it's supposed to be. We might recall some funny thing or profound event connecting us with that particular person. They might remember something you did or said; all the while you've totally forgotten it, only now in this moment, you recall it being good to refresh your memory bank.

Things just pass away, time will tell what is there, and what is left behind. My son amazes me with his memory, so much better than mine. Reason for me keeping a notebook handy at all times. Some others just recall stuff that stuck in their minds and if we're lucky we were part of it.

Folks have a way of slipping into our lives and out of our lives...we are like sand on the beach....shifting and shining in the moonlight as long as the time we have on this earth, knowing full well we only have so much time to share with the ones who will soon be gone away. As somebody once said, 'I'm picking up what you're putting down.'

========= 30 =========